RICHARD WAGNER *His Lucerne period   The museum in Tribschen*

RICHARD WAGNER

His Lucerne period   The museum in Tribschen

Keller & Co AG, Publishers, Lucerne

Front Cover:
Franz Stassen (1869–1949),
painter, graphic artist, stage designer,
friend of Siegfried Wagner: Tryptich
"Tristan and Isolde", inner face (circa 1916)

Back Cover:

Richard Wagner, portrait in oils.
Copy by Margarethe von Bobecker,
from the original by Franz von Lenbach
(circa 1876)

Our thanks are due to the following,
for making the production of this book possible:

Richard Wagner Museum, Lucerne
Gertrud Kappeler, Custodian
Werner Lehmann, Director

Lucerne Record Office
Edgar Rüesch, Keeper of Public Records

The Central Library Lucerne
Pictorial Archives

© 1983 by Keller & Co AG, Publishers, Lucerne

Official Guidebook
of the Richard Wagner Museum, Lucerne

Production:
Keller & Co AG, Printers and Publishers, CH-6002 Lucerne

Editorial and texts:
Dr. Othmar Fries, Dr. Michael Riedler, Dr. Fritz Schaub,
Peter A. Meyer

Translation: McKean Taylor

Pictures and reproductions: Peter A. Meyer

Realization: Peter I. Joho

Layout: Ernst Schmachtenberg

Printed in Switzerland
ISBN 3-85766-006-6

City of Lucerne official guidebook of the Richard Wagner Museum

MICHAEL RIEDLER
Richard Wagner and Lucerne

WAGNER'S VISITS TO LUCERNE PRIOR TO THE TRIBSCHEN YEARS

Wagner had already established more than a passing acquaintanceship with Lucerne and its surroundings before he took up residence in the Tribschen villa, having visited the town on *four occasions* previously. The *first* of these was on *28th August 1850*. From May 1849 Wagner, as a political refugee, lived in exile in Zurich. As a result of his revolutionary sympathies and the part he had played in the Dresden uprising, there was a warrant out for him, and he would have been arrested immediately had he returned to Germany. Thus he was prevented from being present at the first performance of "Lohengrin", conducted by Franz Liszt, at Weimar. Instead, he an his wife Minna, who suffered from heart disease, undertook an excursion to the Rigi and on the return journey they stopped over at the hotel "Schwanen" in Lucerne. Here, from far away, he participated, in his thoughts, at the premiere of his opera, whereby, with watch in hand, he followed "exactly the moment of its beginning and that surmised moment of its end".[1]

In *July 1854* Wagner came to Lucerne again. He had been invited by the Federal Music As-sociation to take over the direction of the music festival in Sitten for that year. This he had declined to do, but had promised "to conduct Beethoven's 7th Symphony on one of the festival days". Arriving in the Valais, he was confronted "contrary to all expectation" with "completely trivial and undertaking". Appall-ed by the "sound of the extremely meagre orchestra" and "indignant at the thoughtlessness which sought to involve him in such an occasion" he departed at once without even so much as an adieu. By way of Berne and Lucerne he travelled to Seelisberg above the Lake of Lucerne, where his wife was taking medical treatment in the form of a whey cure.[2]

Wagner's third visit to Lucerne was in *May 1858*. Whilst working in Zurich on "Tristan and Isolde" he received an invitation from the *Grand Duke Karl Alexander of Weimar* to meet him in Lucerne, where the prince, returning from his travels in Italy, had broken his journey. The purpose of the meeting was to discuss the question of an amnesty for the composer, thereby enabling him to return to Germany. Wagner was received in the most friendly manner, but the discussion brought no tangible results and he had to go back to Zurich without having achieved anything.[3]

In the *Spring of 1859* Wagner once again found himself in Lucerne, the fourth visit. He had been in Venice and left it when fighting broke out between the Austrians and the Risorgimento, the Italian freedom movement. As he could not return to Zurich because of his amorous entanglement with Frau Wesendonck, wife of his Zurich host, he put up at the hotel "Schweizerhof" on 29th March and lodged there until his departure on 7th September. He describes his reception at the "Schweizerhof": "Colonel Segesser, the hospitable proprietor of the hotel, placed a whole floor of the left annexe at my disposal and I was able to install myself very comfortably at little cost in the principle apartments. My only concern was to find a suitable domestic attendant, as the hotel at that period was but modestly equipped in this respect; and here I had the good fortune to acquire the services of a conscientious young female who proved truly devoted to my welfare and whose good care of me, especially in the later season when the hotel became more lively, gave me cause to remember her, and many years afterwards, as a consequence, to appoint her as my housekeeper."[4] The "young female" was *Vreneli Weidmann* who, together with her future husband Jakob Stocker, was to belong to the personnel of the Tribschen "court".

The continually wet and bitterly cold weather was a great trial to Wagner. More oppressive still was the fact that the work of composing was not making the headway he had expected. In order to improve his poor health and relieve nervous tension he made it a habit of going out for a morning ride: "My host lent me for this exercise a 25-year old horse called Lise; on this animal I rode out every morning for just so long as it pleased her to amble forwards: she never carried me very far but resolutely turned back at certain places, without paying the slightest heed to my equestrian admonitions."[5] Shortly before the completion of "Tristan and Isolde", full of high spirits, he "composed" a nonsense verse on one of these morning rides and sang it to his maid Vreneli Weidmann afterwards. Freely translated it goes something like this:

"In Lucerne's 'Schweizerhof',
Far from house and home,
Tristan and Isolde died,
Sad was he and she was fair,
Died they gladly, free as air,
In 'Schweizerhof' of Lucerne,
Held by Colonel Segesser(n)."[6]

How the Lucernese reacted to Wagner at that time is indicated by a contemporary account: "I listened to him sometimes–the windows were open–on my way home at eleven o'clock. There were those eccentric music figures, peculiar to him, which make such violent leaps, not to everyone's taste… On several occasions early in the morning… I saw the composer, who perhaps had been working the night through, pacing slowly up and down the narrow balcony of the first floor, whether relaxing or meditating–it could have been both. But that was not it which interested me, rather the fantastic costume: a long, deer-coloured (reddish-violet) dressing gown and headgear of the same tones, shaped after the old German façon. With his hands clasped behind his back, head erect, and slow measured tread–he seemed oblivious of life around him, of the passers-by on the street, of the steamers leaving the quay."[7]

At the beginning of the summer season, Wagner moved from the annexe to the second floor of the main building, as there were no permanent guests there, only those staying for a short time, who used their rooms merely for sleeping. Commenting on this removal, he said: "As it proved, this arrangement turned out to be surprisingly good: from then on I could work completely undisturbed in my smaller living-room and bedchamber, for the other rooms on this floor taken by strangers were only used at night for sleeping and were thus completely unoccupied during the day. At last the summer came, truly sumptuous weather lasting for two whole months, every day cloudless skies. I savoured that peculiar magic of the breaking of the sun's extremest blaze by cultivating coolness and semi-darkness in my room, while only at evening time did I give myself wholly to the efficacy of the summer air, sitting on my little balcony. There I had great pleasure in listening to some accomplished hornplayers, who, with great regularity, on board a skiff on the lake, gave charming performances of simple folksongs.– And happily, in my work I had now unravelled the terrible Gordian Knot…"[8]

At the end of July Wagner received a visit from the 23-year old composer *Felix Draeseke,* who kept him company for four weeks. Draeseke's notes give us an insight into the life and creative work of Wagner's during this fourth stay in Lucerne.[9] Draeseke describes for example, how Wagner finished the Tristan score: "At six in the evening I came to him and was received with the words: 'Wait a moment, the 'Tristan' is just being completed.' 'I must be present at that', I said, and experienced how the beautiful introductory motif flowed into the glorious B Major chord and the tones of the full orchestra were painted in an astonishingly brief space of time. When I noticed that in this last chord the tuba employed earlier was missing and I en-

quired after the reason, he said to me: 'What use are the old villain's grunts now?' Artistically he was absolutely right, for without this uncouth instrument the end sounded much nobler."

Wagner and Draeseke made a number of excursions in the region, for example to Brunnen, on the Rigi, to the Rütli and Tell's Chapel. As the boat in which they sat neared the chapel, Wagner told Draeseke to shout as loudly as he could to awaken the echo from the chapel. The young man being reluctant to do so, Wagner bellowed out all kinds of curses into the air, and was highly amused by the lingering responses. Together also they climbed the Pilatus, Wagner, unlike his companion, proving to be very skillful, with absolutely no fear of heights and risking passages that even experienced mountaineers regarded as dangerous.

When the *Wesendonck couple* visited Wagner at the "Schweizerhof", the master gave them a foretaste of 'Tristan and Isolde'. Draeseke has left us the following account: "Wagner played the second act of 'Tristan' for them, in that characteristic manner of his, that is he raced up and down the piano keys, added vocal accompaniment, unfortunately all too often out of tune, sweated, worked himself into a passion, in short, gave a performance that no way resembled what one could expect from a thoroughly well-trained practical musician. Yet he had a gift, shining through a veil as it were, of explaining his intentions and making the dramatic situations and the various characters recognizable."

With the completion of "Tristan and Isolde" Wagner's fourth visit to Lucerne likewise approached its end. On 7th September 1859 he started on his journey to Paris, which he reached on 15th September after two brief stops on the way, the first in Zurich at the Wesendoncks' and the second in Winterthur at the Sulzers'.

THE TRIBSCHEN YEARS

Wagner's fifth and final stay in Lucerne lasted from *1st April 1866 to 22nd April 1872.*
All his biographers agree that Wagner's time in Tribschen was the happiest and most fruitful period of his life. In those six years his fortunes changed for the better, something he had hardly dared hope for. By his marriage he legalized his relationship to Cosima–a relationship that had shocked and offended many. The birth of a daughter and a son completed the Tribschen family idyll. And the money worries that had dogged his footsteps for so long were dispersed by the enthusiastic generosity of the young king of Bavaria, Ludwig II. Free from all such external problems, Wagner could devote his energies to musical and literary creation amidst the peaceful, secluded surroundings of his country mansion.

The Arrival at Tribschen
Wagner had been forced to leave Munich the previous year, his departure the consequence of a bitter and virulent press campaign against him, and settled down first in the neighbourhood of Geneva. Travelling from Geneva over Lausanne, Berne and Interlaken, Richard Wagner and his companion, *Cosima von Bülow,* reached Lucerne on Good Friday, 30th March 1866. During a boat trip on the lake, they discovered the Tribschen villa, at that time in a rather neglected state. While Cosima continued her journey to Munich, Wagner returned to Geneva briefly to make the necessary arrangements for the change in domicile. On the Tuesday after Easter he took a room at the "Schweizerhof" and concluded an agreement with the owner of the Tribschen estate, *Lt.-Col. Walter Am Rhyn,* to take the property on lease for one year at a rental of Sfr. 3000. The house was furnished–according to contract, all that the tenant was required to bring was bedlinen, table-linen and kitchen towels.[10] In the "Luzern Zeitung" of 13th April, the front page carried the announcement: "This summer Lucerne will experience the pleasure of having the well-known composer of 'music of the future', Richard Wagner, in its midst or at least nearby. The same has rented the beautifully situated country house Tribschen for a lengthy stay."
Wagner, who was accustomed to living in a big way, now set about with bewildering energy to put his new home in order according to his taste. As the existing furnishings did not suit him, he ordered replacements by telegraph from Geneva, Munich and Vienna. In addition he had a number of structural alterations made in the house itself. An army of workmen, local and imported, had to fulfil his wishes within the shortest possible time. And for once Wagner had no financial problems, because his devoted admirer and patron, Ludwig II of Bavaria, not only paid the rent but supplied him with funds for living expenses. Wagner was able to move in already on 15th April, and Cosima followed on the 12th May.

The Wagner Familiy in Tribschen
During the first years in Tribschen Wagner's private affairs were in a very muddled state. His partner Cosima was still officially married to the pianist and conductor Hans von Bülow, who had resigned himself to the loss of his

wife's affections and yet had the strength of character and nobility of spirit to remain an enthusiastic admirer and champion of Wagner's music. Although in fact Cosima had in her heart already decided for Wagner, circumstances and a sense of duty and the proprieties forced her to leave Wagner from time to time and accompany her husband to Munich or Basle. Both Wagner and Cosima made every effort to conceal the fact of their liaison, but it became more and more public property. At first Ludwig II brushed aside the rumours as malicious and absurd, for he had a blind faith in Wagner and Cosima, whose protestations of innocence he accepted completely. All the more bitter his disappointment when in spring 1869 he learnt the truth. On November 16th, 1866, Cosima, accompanied by her daughters Isolde and Eva, moved in with Wagner permanently at Tribschen. In her diary, which she was writing for her children, there is the following entry: "The year 1868 marks the decisive turning-point in my life, in this year it was granted me to fulfil what for five years has been my soul's desire. I have not sought after this fulfilment, nor caused it–it has been laid upon me by destiny."[11]

Isolde, born on 10th April 1865 in Munich, was not Bülow's child, but the first tangible result of the liaison between Cosima and Wagner. The second child, *Eva,* was born on 17th February 1867 in Tribschen. In the Register of Births she was entered as being the "legitimate daughter of Hans von Bülow, Royal Prussian Kapellmeister (music conductor), domiciled in Lucerne, and of Cosima Franziska Liszt."[12]

On 6th June 1869, *Siegfried,* first and only son, was born. The event is commemorated in her diary:

"O blest the day that surrounds us with light, blest the sun that shines down upon us! Alas, poor me, how can I find expression for the feelings with which I open this book again? When the midwife told me: 'My best wishes, ma'am, it's a boy', I had to laugh and cry and pray. Dear God, You who gave him to me, keep him safe, he is the protector of his sisters, his adored father's heir."[13]

Nine days after the birth, Cosima, in a letter to Hans von Bülow, asked for a divorce and begged him also to give her the custody of *Daniela and Blandine,* their two legitimate daughters. Bülow agreed, and the wearisome process of dissolving a Catholic marriage finally ended in the Berlin court on 18th July 1870, with a decision in favour of the defendants. Nothing now stood in the way of a marriage between Cosima and Wagner. After the authorities in Leipzig had sent the necessary documents, the Lucerne Executive Council announced its decision:

"Concerning the application of the composer Wilhelm Richard Wagner of Leipzig, for permission to enter the holy state of matrimony in the Canton of Lucerne with Franziska Cosima, formerly von Bülow, née Liszt, of Berlin, the Executive Council having taken into consideration

– that the authorities of the bridegroom's native land have given the latter permission to form a union abroad,

– the just observance of the laws pertaining to the licensing and consecration of marriages, has resolved:

1. The said applicant, upon publication of the banns at the incumbency concerned, is herewith granted leave to enter into a state of wedlock with his betrothed, in the Canton of Lucerne.

2. This present permission which remains valid for 2 months, is to be notified to the applicant."[14]

The wedding was celebrated by *Pastor Johann Heinrich Tschudi* on 28th August 1870 in the Protestant church of St. Mathew's in Lucerne. The witnesses were *Malwida von Meysenbug* and *Hans Richter*. Cosima wrote in her diary afterwards: "May I be worthy to bear Richard's name! My prayers have concentrated on two things alone: Richard's well-being, to be there always for it; and that Hans, far away from me, may lead a serene and happy life."[15] And in remembrance of his wedding-day, Wagner endowed the Protestant parish of Lucerne with an annual payment of 50 francs. Their son, Siegfried, now over a year old, was not baptized until after the marriage. The ceremony took place on 4th September 1870, the child received the names *Helferich Siegfried Richard*. Godparents were *Ludwig II of Bavaria* and the *Countess Caroline Waldbott-Bassenheim* of Bavaria.

Certainly Richard Wagner felt secure in Tribschen, in the peaceful stillness and solitude of its surroundings. But he had not the slightest intention of cutting himself off from the world or of denying himself the amenities of a well-ordered household appropriate to his position.

At times his "court" counted upward of a dozen persons: Cosima with the two daughters from her marriage with Hans von Bülow, then their own children, further their staff, namely a governess, a nurserymaid, a housekeeper, a cook and two or three servants. To it also belonged a small "zoo": Wagner's black Newfoundland "Russ" and Cosima's grey fox-terrier "Koss" (Cosima had given the dog this name, in order to stop people from using the abbreviation "Cos" for her), further the horse "Fritz", then sheep, hens and cats, as well as a pair of golden pheasants and the pair of peacocks Cosima had brought from Munich, "Wotan" and "Fricka".

Also a member of this "court" was the young *Hans Richter,* who had taken up his duties as Wagner's secretary and copyist on 30th October 1866. Richter, who had played the horn in the orchestra of the Royal Opera in Vienna, was not only active as a musical secretary, but also as maître de plaisir, organizing house concerts in Tribschen, and he became a close friend of the whole Wagner family.

Guests in Tribschen
Wagner kept open house in Tribschen, receiving many illustrious guests, above all his devoted admirer and patron Ludwig II of Bavaria. On 22nd May 1866, Wagner's 53rd birthday, Ludwig arrived quite unexpectedly in Tribschen, giving his name at the door as Walther von Stolzing. Two days later he returned to Munich. The indignation in the capital at this secretive departure was widespread. That, at a time when his country was involved on the Austrian side in the war between Prussia and Austria, the king had nothing better to do than to visit his musical favourite and debtor aroused great resentment.

The poet Georg Herwegh, who had early on recognized the genius of Wagner and saw in him not only the musician but the democrat and revolutionary, and honoured him for it, parodied this episod in his "Ballad of the Lost King":

"In Bavaria, Bavaria,
The king has run away;
Missing and forgotten,
For practically a day;
For his folk, there's the sting–
What can one do without a king?"

In the succeeding verses he describes how the king in his thoughts takes leave of his cabinet ministers in a mocking fashion, and then he continues:

"Groom rode with master,
Via Zurich to Lucerne,
Happy in the land of Tell's
Blessed with hotels.
The master spoke: Tell est mon plaisir
And Richard Wagner find I here.

Greetings to you, tone-jewel,
Better than a crown-jewel,
I'll stay in your villa.
Is not today dies illa,
That life to you once gave,
To frighten the 'old guard' into the grave?"

Finally he depicts the confusion and chaos that had broken out in the Cabinet at Munich and turns then to the king:

"The Prince feasts with the Troubadour,
In Major and Minor, Minor and Major,
With his nightgear he carries,
No sceptre or crown,
And only the third day remembers–viz.:
That he the king of Bavaria is."

The poem ends with the safe return of the monarch to his capital, welcomed by his cheering subjects.

Wagner's presence made Tribschen into a veritable place of pilgrimage for his disciples and admirers. There was a constant coming and going of famous personalities. Among those who especially deserve to be singled out for mention were his musician friends, the composers *Franz Liszt,* Cosima's father, and *Peter Cornelius,* then the pianist *Josef Rubinstein,* the music scholar *Edouard Schuré,* the architect *Gottfried Semper,* and the poet-philosopher *Friedrich Nietzsche,* who was a regular visitor to Tribschen from 1866 on. His 23 visits testify to the lively exchange of ideas between the young philosophy professor from Basel University and the mature master. In "Ecce homo" Nietzsche wrote: "Not for anything in the world would I trade away those days of my life spent in Tribschen–days of trust, of serenity and brightness, of sublime happenings–of profound moments... I do not know what the experience of others has been with Wagner: in our heavens there was never a cloud."[17] This friendship did not last–Nietzsche was later to pursue Wagner with a bitter hatred.

Other distinguished guests were the French writers *Judith Gautier* and her husband *Catulle Mendès* as well as their mutual friend, the poet *Villiers de l'Isle Adam.* Their arrival in July 1869 caused something of a stir in Lucerne. Met by Wagner at the railway station the three travellers were taken to the Hotel du Lac, where Wagner had reserved rooms for them. They soon noticed that the hotel staff treated them with especial deference; whenever they went out they were stared after with the greatest interest and everywhere people greeted them with exaggerated respect. Catulle Mendès, thoroughly irritated by all this, asked the hotel director what the fuss was about, and discovered that they had been mistaken for three other personages, namely, Ludwig II, the Count of Taxis and the opera singer Adelina Patti. Wagner found it very amusing. "You see now", he told his "chère Trinité", "you have not only touched our hearts, hardened to human wickedness, you've also turned the heads of the Lucernese who are normally very apathetic."[18]

Wagner and the Citizens

Wagner soon became a familiar figure to the people of Lucerne. As the Police Commissioner gravely reported, he behaved like any other citizen, and as he was not "incommoded" in any way, there was no need to give him police protection.

Every afternoon at three, Wagner would put on his immense and rather alarming "Wotan" hat and go out for a walk with his dog. He usually went into the town where there was often shopping to do: he collected the mail, rummaged around Schiffmann's antiquarian bookshop in the Krongasse, bought delicious things at Häcki's, the confectioner's in the Weggisgasse, his footwear at Jules Coulin's in the same street, had his hair cut at Mauritz Stoll's saloon in the Kapellgasse, and whenever he required manuscripts or books to be bound or repaired, would have this done by the bookbinder Wilhelm Schläpfer in the Werchlaube. Affable and gregarious he would often chat to the tradespeople and craftsmen for hours on end, but they also got to know the other side of his nature. Extravagant and generous when it came to the luxuries that were essential to his artistic temperament, he was miserly about spending money on the everyday necessities. "Mean as the devil" would be the summing-up of the cautiously expressed verdict of those who mainly knew this side of him–"Thriftiness bordering on the impermissible". And he was an awful "stickler and difficult to please". He frequently got people's backs up in this respect. One day, at Anton Eglin's shop in the Kapellgasse, where he would buy his stationery and music paper, he practically turned the shop upside down and drove the saleswoman frantic in his search for a suitable pen. Finally he bought one, but was back the next day, demanding to have it exchanged as it was of no earthly use. The woman lost her temper, there were high words between them, but Wagner's were louder, more colourful and more offensive, so at last the desirability of his never darkening those particular doors again was pointed out to him. The following afternoon he collared Herr Eglin: "Your shopgirl was confoundedly rude to me yesterday." "Shopgirl!" cried Eglin, "that was my wife, and if I'd been there I'd have told you the same damned thing!" Unruffled, and always willing to forgive lesser mortals he had injured, Wagner continued to shop there.

His business done, Wagner would go into the "Dubeli" pub in the Furrengasse before going home. Here–it is now a Chinese restaurant–he would drink his beer, read the newspapers and talk with the other guests.

He struck up a friendship with the Lucerne artist *Josef Zelger,* whose landscape paintings glorified the beauties of the Alps. Zelger had set up his studio in the garden of the hotel "Schweizerhof" and received friends and clients there, including many prominent visitors. One of these was Wagner, to whom the artist presented a painting. In return Wagner gave him the Minnesänger-watch he himself had received as a Christmas present from Ludwig II in 1864, a signed photograph of himself with a dedication, and a morocco leather-bound copy

14

of the "Meistersinger". Zelger was also invited to dinner at Tribschen.[20]

There was little close contact between Wagner and the music life in Lucerne. Understandably–Lucerne was then, musically speaking, wrapped in darkness.[21] True, a municipal theatre had existed since 1839 but for financial reasons had to serve up popular pieces: *circenses* for the public meant *panem* for the theatre. Like faint lights in the darkness, amateur groups put on performances of contemporary opera, badly done, of course, but pointers in the right direction. And Wagner had friendly contact with *Gustav Arnold,* the Lucerne Music Director, who introduced public chamber music concerts as a first step towards musical professionalism in Lucerne. For these concerts Arnold engaged musicians from outside, who were competent and well-trained and he also "borrowed" from Wagner the services of Hans Richter, not only a masterly hornplayer but one who could perform on all the other orchestral instruments necessary.[22]

On his 57th birthday Wagner was treated to a touching gesture of Lucerne's goodwill. Cosima had taken up contact with *Gregor Lampert,* the conductor of the Lucerne Brass Band, some time before, and had suggested that the band should play a birthday serenade for her husband. On the Sunday morning, May 22nd, 1870, Wagner awoke to the sound of his Homage March that he had composed for Ludwig II's 19th birthday in 1864. A great crowd had assembled before the house, all those who, impelled by curiosity or deeper feelings, had come to pay their respects. Profoundly moved, Wagner thanked conductor and musicians individually shaking hands and clinking the wine-glass with all.[23]

During the Tribschen period Wagner had often discussed theatre projects with the architect *Gottfried Semper,* designer of the Dresden State Opera House. His great dream was to have a theatre built purely for his works. He also contemplated doing this in Lucerne and broached the theme to the Lucerne architect *Joseph Placidus von Segesser,* imagining that the latter, an influential and highly respected citizen, would have no difficulty in raising the financial means required. Again and again he begged the architect to produce some plans, but von Segesser, who considered Wagner's idea to be completely unrealistic and impracticable, refused to touch the project.

Wagner's Creative Work in Tribschen

As already mentioned, the Tribschen years were among the most fruitful of Wagner's life as far as musical creation was concerned. Here in the happy family circle, the master found that inner peace and concentration that enabled him to work on his great music dramas.

In December 1870 Wagner had secretly composed a serenade for Cosima's birthday. This "Tribschen Idyll" as he first named it became known throughout the world later as the "Siegfried Idyll". The preparations for its performance and the rehearsals were of course also kept strictly secret from Cosima. Hans Richter was organizing the surprise. He rehearsed the music with 15 players of the Zurich Theatre Orchestra, played the trumpet part himself and practised in the Lucerne Barracks on a borrowed instrument, in order not to arouse curiosity in Tribschen over his activities. Cosima became extremely suspicious about his many visits to Zurich and frequent absences from the house and she told her husband she thought Richter was losing interest in his job. After the general rehearsal in the Lucerne Hotel du Lac, conducted by Wagner, the musicians came to Tribschen very early in the morning of the 25th December, 1870, tuned their instruments in the spacious kitchen and took up their positions on the staircase: For the first time the beautiful melodies of the "Siegfried Idyll" sounded through the house. Cosima tried to put down in her diary the impressions and feelings she experienced at receiving this unique birthday present, and the very inadequacy of her expression is the greatest testimony to the profundity of those feelings: "My children, I can tell you nothing of what I felt on this day, nothing about my mood, nothing, nothing at all. Only an arid and colourless account of what happened: As I awoke I heard a sound that became fuller and richer, I knew it was not a dream, it was music I heard, and what music! As the sounds died away Richard came into my room with the five children and presented me with the score of the 'Symphonic Birthday Greetings'–I was in tears, but so was the whole house; Richard had placed his orchestra on the stairway and so consecrated for ever our Tribschen!"[25]

The "Stair music", as the children called it, was repeated several times that day at Cosima's request. At first it was her exclusive property and she regarded it as a most intimate memory of that eventful stay with Wagner at the Starnberg Lake in July 1864.

In 1871 Wagner composed the "Emperor March" in honour of the founding of the Second German Empire. In Tribschen he finished the score of the "Meistersinger von Nürnberg". Then, after an interval of twelve years, he took up the interrupted work on the "Ring" cycle. He completed the "Siegfried" in 1871 with the composition of the third act, and began on the "Twilight of the Gods". While in Lucerne he finished the orchestration sketches for the 1st and 2nd acts, and the composition sketch for the 3rd act of this, the last part of the great drama.

It was not only musical creation, however, that filled Wagner's working days at Tribschen. He devoted a great deal of his time and energy to his literary activities, and in addition to numerous smaller works, he produced here four of his major cultural studies: "German Art and German Politics", 1868; "On Conducting", 1869; the great "Beethoven", 1870, and "The Nature of Opera", 1871. Two famous earlier treatises, "Judaism in Music" (1850) and "Opera and Drama" (1850/51) were brought out in new editions. And besides all this he dictated to Cosima his autobiography "My Life" which covered the tumultuous years up to 1864. Cosima herself conscientiously filled her Tribschen journals with all that happened during their residence there. Wagner's own diary, the "Brown Book" given to him by Cosima, was begun in 1865 and he carried it on in Tribschen–it gives us an insight into all the ideas and inspirations that guided and motivated him.

Departure from Tribschen

Wagner had never lost sight of his great aim to have his own festival theatre in which his works could be performed exactly as he wanted them to be. After having to abandon his plans for the building of such a theatre in Munich, largely for political reasons, he and his wife travelled to Bayreuth in April 1871, a town he had long been considering as fitted for his purpose. The decision was made: Wagner had found the right place and immediately began with plans, not only for the building of a theatre which would house his festival, but also for a home for himself and his family. The Bayreuth Corporation placed a building site at his disposal for the first project–the theatre– and on 1st February 1872 Wagner purchased a plot of land on which his home, the villa "Wahnfried", was to be built–the Wagners moved in there in 1874. The festival Committee was set up and the hunt for financial patronage was on–although the foundation stone of the Bayreuth Festival Theatre was ceremoniously laid on the 22nd of May 1872, and Ludwig II's Treasury was the principle donator, the inaugural performance of the "Ring" did not take place until 1876.

The excitement of the foundation ceremony on the 22nd May–Wagner's 59th birthday–must certainly have partly dispelled the melancholy that the departure from Tribschen had caused. For a month previously, on 22nd April, Wagner had said his last farewells to his Lucerne home, and Cosima and the children had followed him at the end of the same month. The Tribschen years were over. Yet, perhaps, it was the hidden merit of time and the course of events, that the name "Tribschen Idyll" could truly be given to this whole period of their lives, and remain true for them afterwards, for their family and their friends, for the world at large ever since.

The desolation of leave-taking was described by Cosima in a letter to her friend, Marie von Schleinitz: "It hurts Wagner terribly, and this touches the very mainspring of my being. Giving up our idyllic existence here is more difficult and painful than many people imagine..."[26] Nietzsche witnessed the folding of the tents. He had come to Tribschen on April 25th to see Wagner once more and found only Cosima and the servants in the process of packing up: "So Tribschen has ceased to exist! We walked about as if among the ruins. Sadness hung in the air, in the clouds; the dog refused to eat, the servants, when one spoke to them, answered in tears. We packed the manuscripts, letters and books together–oh, it was all so bleak!"[27]

(Notes: see German version.)

NOTES

[1] Richard Wagner: Mein Leben. Vollständige, kommentierte Ausgabe, hg. von Martin Gregor-Dellin. München 1976. S. 465.

[2] Wagner, Mein Leben, S. 519 ff.

[3] Wagner, Mein Leben, S. 578 f.

[4] Wagner, Mein Leben, S. 599.

[5] Wagner, Mein Leben, S. 602.

[6] Brief von Richard Wagner an Mathilde Wesendonck vom 9. Juli 1859. In: Richard Wagner an Mathilde Wesendonck. Tagebuchblätter und Briefe 1853–1871. Berlin 1904. S. 157 ff.

[7] Anton Schürmann: Handschriftliche Aufzeichnungen. Erinnerungen, Biographisches, Historisches. Band 1 (Zentralbibliothek Luzern).

[8] Wagner, Mein Leben, S. 603.

[9] Felix Draeseke und Richard Wagner in Luzern. Aus den unveröffentlichen Lebenserinnerungen. In: Der kleine Bund, Nrn. 43 u. 44, 28. Okt. u. 4. Nov. 1923.

[10] Max Fehr: Richard Wagners Schweizer Zeit. Band 2. Aarau 1953. S. 425.

[11] Cosima Wagner: Die Tagebücher. Ediert und kommentiert von Martin Gregor-Dellin und Dietrich Mack. Band 1 (1869–1877). München 1976. S. 21.

[12] Louis Zimmermann: Richard Wagner in Luzern. Berlin 1910. S. 109.

[13] Cosima Wagner, Tagebücher, S. 107.

[14] Verhandlungsprotokoll des Regierungsrates des Kantons Luzern vom 22. 8. 1870. In: Zimmermann, Wagner in Luzern, S. 134 f.

[15] Cosima Wagner, Tagebücher, S. 277.

[16] Adolf Zinsstag: Die Briefsammlungen des Richard-Wagner-Museums in Tribschen bei Luzern. Basel 1961. S. 64.

[17] Friedrich Nietzsche: Werke. Kritische Gesamtausgabe, 6. Abt., Band 3. Berlin 1969. S. 286 (5. Kapitel im Abschnitt «Warum ich so klug bin»).

[18] Alois Weber: Judith Gautier, Catulle Mendès und Villiers de l'Adam bei Richard Wagner in Tribschen. In: Der Geschichtsfreund, 102 (1949), S. 159 ff.

[19] Schürmann, Aufzeichnungen, Band 1.

[20] Franz Zelger: Landschaftsmalerei und aufblühender Fremdenverkehr – der Beitrag Josef Zelgers. In: Luzern 1178–1978; Beiträge zur Geschichte der Stadt. Luzern 1978. S. 429 ff.

[21] Othmar Fries: Luzerns Musikleben im 10. und 20. Jahrhundert. In: Der Geschichtsfreund, 112 (1959), S. 184 ff.

[22] Gustav Arnold: Handschriftliche Aufzeichnungen. Autobiographische Notizen. Heft 1 (Zentralbibliothek Luzern).

[23] Brief von Cosima Wagner an Friedrich Nietzsche vom 23. Mai 1870. In: Zinsstag, Briefsammlungen, S. 55 f.

[24] Diese Angaben stammen vom Urenkel des Joseph Placidus von Segesser, Dr. Hans-Ulrich von Segesser (gest. 30. Juli 1982).

[25] Cosima Wagner, Tagebücher, S. 329.

[26] Richard Wagner in Selbstzeugnissen und im Urteil der Zeitgenossen. Zusammengestellt und hg. von Martin Hürlimann. Zürich 1972. S. 264 f.

[27] Brief von Friedrich Nietzsche an Carl von Gersdorff vom 1. Mai 1872. In: Friedrich Nietzsche: Briefwechsel. Kritische Gesamtausgabe. 2. Abt., Band 1. Berlin 1977. S. 315 ff.

FRITZ SCHAUB
The Tribschen Museum

FROM RESIDENCE TO MUSEUM

Richard Wagner's ties with Tribschen were always to remain a strong emotional element in his later life, although he only visited it once after his departure in 1872. That was five years later when, on his way home from London with his whole family, he stopped at Lucerne on 19th July 1877. The villa had been deserted and unoccupied for the first few years but was now the home of a French family, who tactfully withdrew on this occasion to allow their famous guest to be alone with his memories. It must have been a most moving experience for parents and children as they walked through the old familiar rooms that, in spite of everything, were still theirs in a spiritual sense. Wieland Wagner, Richard's grandson, whose all too early death deprived Bayreuth of a brilliant producer and interpreter of the Wagner operas, has left us, in his essay "From Tribschen to Wahnfried", a description of the moment: "Wagner was silent and pensive. Only once did the mood change, a sarcastic smile played over his lips. Lying open on the grand piano was a pianoforte arrangement–of Meyerbeer's 'The Hugenots'…"[1]

More than 20 years later Cosima returned to Tribschen. It was in 1905 that she was able to send the faithful Hans Richter greetings from herself and Vreneli in Tribschen "where we saw the Meistersinger room". Eight years later she paid another brief visit, this time with her daughters. "We spent a day in Lucerne to see Vreneli and Tribschen. How this once peaceful town has changed beyond recognition! The ugliness of the railway station and the hotel under the lowering skies was a nightmare and apparition. But the whole Tribschen side is untouched and my walk there with Eva in the silvery light was lovely as a dream."

Not long after Wagner's death the Tribschen tenancy changed hands, this time an English family took possession, and from then on the turnover of occupancy was frequent–sometimes it was let for the summer season, a month at a time. Strangers on pilgrimage, from all parts of the world, often stood before a closed and shuttered silence… And then in Lucerne, in 1929, a commission was set up, whose aim was the transformation of the Tribschen mansion into a museum commemorating Wagner. The energetic initiative of the mayor of Lucerne at that time, Dr. Jakob Zimmerli, resulted in the purchase of the Tribschen estate by the city in 1931. The property, consisting of the villa and the 30,000 sq.m. park surrounding it, the entail inheritance of the Am Rhyn family, was transferred to the city of Lucerne for the sum of Sfr. 275,000. As entail land is in principle unsaleable, the Lucerne Greater Council had to give its authorization for the change in its nature–from land to cash. On 1th July 1933 the memorial to Wagner–the only one in Switzerland–was ceremoniously inaugurated. On 5th April 1956 the "Richard Wagner Tribschen Museum" Association, under the chairmanship of the city mayor, Paul Kopp, was founded. Its purpose was the maintenance, preservation and furtherance both of the Tribschen mansion and the works of Wagner. Later, the society altered its name to that of the "Swiss Richard Wagner Association".

Even though Tribschen was now officially a museum, it retained the character of a home–of Wagner's home. The first floor was reserved for the use of the members of his family, that is the children of Siegfried and Winifred Wagner, as well as the two Wagner daughters, Eva Chamberlain-Wagner (1867–1942) and Daniela Thode-von Bülow (1860–1940). Eva and Daniela were regular visitors each year for a few weeks in summer, between 1934 and 1939. Their gratitude for this gesture of the Lucerne authorities expressed itself in generous gifts of Wagneriana for the museum. And Baron Hans von Wolzogen, Count Biagio and Countess Blandine Gravina as well as Siegfried's two daughters, Verena (born 1920) and Friedelind (born 1918) often came there. Friedelind stayed for seven months at Tribschen after the outbreak of the Second World War, having refused to return to her family in Germany. Well-looked after by the custodian, Frau Ellen Beerli, the predecessor of Frau Gertrud Kapeler, she was accommodated in the large, first-floor apartment that had formerly been Cosima's salon, the room that Daniela von Bülow used on her summer visits. On 1st March 1940 Friedelind Wagner left Tribschen and Switzerland for New York, which she reached via London and Buenos Aires, and where she was welcomed with open arms and friendly offers of assistance. After the last direct descendant of Wagner, Eva Chamberlain, died in 1942, the apartment in the first floor was transformed into a display section for old musical instruments, the collection of Heinrich Schumacher-Scheidegger, which had been purchased by the city of Lucerne in 1943 at the instigation of the architect Otto Dreyer, an expert on the subject.

Behind the house a memorial by the Lucerne sculptor Alfred Peyer reminds us that Tribschen was also, in a sense, the birthplace of the Lucerne International Music Festival. It carries the following inscription: "Arturio Toscanini, freeman of the city of Lucerne, conducted in this park on 25th August 1938 works by Mozart, Beethoven, Rossini and Wagner."

It is worth mentioning in this connection that the incomparable "Siegfried Idyll" was again heard in the place where it had been created, although not this time on the staircase within, but outside in the park in the version scored for large orchestra and under the baton of the Italian maestro, who with this open-air concert had laid the foundation stone, as it were, of the International Music Festival. Toscanini conducted the "Idyll" once more on 29th August 1939, this taking place inside the house, in what is now Room 4. The audience was gathered outside before the opened windows and only Daniela and Eva were with the orchestra.

Tribschen in Wagner's days

"It is unimaginably beautiful and holy in this place", wrote Wagner in a letter to Heinrich Porges shortly after his moving in to Tribschen on 2nd May 1866. A few days beforehand he had written to the king: "Wherever I turn outside my house I am in the midst of a magic world: I know of no more beautiful place on earth, none homelier than this." And to Frau von Bülow, Wagner depicted the mood at the end of September: "Today Tuesday, a wonderful morning–market day–boats and barges from Uri, Schwyz and Unterwalden on their way to the Lucerne market: A marvellous sight, quite indescribably lovely–each boat on this gentle smooth lake floating within a gleaming circle of silver. A burdensome winter month is not too heavy a price to pay for such a morning."[2]

A coloured pen-and-ink sketch, drawn from nature in the year 1814, hanging in the corridor, near the entrance, fully justifies Wagner's description. But what was Tribschenhorn itself like in Wagner's days? Two contemporary photographs show that the part facing the lake has changed little since his time: on the one photograph we see the boat-house at the lakeside, on the other the extensive wooded park. The hinterland of Tribschen, however, had a different aspect. To the northwest of the villa stood a summerhouse, its exterior finished in birch-bark. It bore the name "Einsiedelei". This must have been the summerhouse referred to by Judith Gautier, the French writer, in her memoirs: "The master led us to a pavilion crowning a rise, from where, as he said, the view was magnificent; the children tumbled about in the soft grass, laughing and squealing with joy. The view was truly enchanting: an undulating sea of green foliage, in which the house seemed to be submerged, billowed from hillock to valley, down to the edge of the clear blue lake, over which a few white sails glided, and whose depths mirrored the violet tones of the high peaks."[3]

This pavilion must still have been standing in 1938, for Julia Virginia Laengsdorff in her long article written after a visit to Tribschen says: "Immediately behind the house, next to a splendid specimen of a Chinese-Japanese 'tree of heaven' (alianthus gladulosa), the small stone pavilion is a reminder of Cosima's existence. Here was her Valhalla."[4]

On the right-hand side of the drive, before it opens out into the forecourt, there is a small hexagonal stone building which in Wagner's time served as an aviary for his peacocks–it is well-known that Wagner's "court" in Tribschen was augmented by what almost amounted to a small private zoo, and the peacock-house was occupied by the pair of peacocks "Wotan" and "Fricka" brought from Munich by Cosima. Richard Wagner also had the so-called "Robbers' Park" laid out, shortly after his arrival. He gave it this name because of a few rocky hollows to which the "Robbers' Path" led. About 200 metres inland stood a farmhouse, in which Wagner's domestic staff Verena Weidmann, Peter Steffen, Jost–and from January 1867, Verena's husband Jakob Stocker lived.[5] To the west side of the villa there were a number of annexes. These included the stable for the old horse "Fritz" (who was joined in 1870 by "Grane", a present from Ludwig II on Wagner's 57th birthday, 22nd May) and, after the alterations made in 1867, the kitchen, laundry-room and coach-house. The main building itself, whose origins probably date back to the Middle Ages, received its present form about 1800.[6] At one time it is said a walled tunnel led

21

from the basement direct to the shore. In Wagner's time a balcony adorned the side of the house facing the lake. This, as well as the annexes, disappeared during the renovation of the property subsequent to its purchase by the city of Lucerne, in 1933.

Let us now turn to the interior of the villa that, like Lucerne farmhouses, is crowned by a widely projecting hip-roof. With its three stories each with five or six rooms, the house provided spacious accommodation for a fair number of persons. During the first period of his stay, Wagner used to work in a room on the first floor. At any rate it was "from above" and not from the ground floor that the tones of the "Meistersinger" wafted down to Cosima's ear as she walked with the children in the garden.[7] Entering the house, one came directly into the kitchen on the right, the adjoining room being the bedroom in which Ludwig II slept for two nights on his only visit to Tribschen. Next to the bedroom was the salon, the main reception room on the ground floor. Continuing in an anti-clockwise direction, one would come to the library-gallery and dining-room on the western side of the house. Already by the spring of 1867 Wagner had initiated far-reaching changes in the layout of the ground floor, and the present arrangement corresponds more or less with the alterations then made. The most important change was removing the kitchen to the annexe; this gave Wagner a small room, that he turned into his bedroom, facing the forecourt and with a view of the Pilatus. The adjoining room was now enlarged, including part of the former kitchen and the former ground floor bedroom, and made into his study. Two walls were lined with books and in 1869 the "working" piano given to him by Ludwig II found its place here. So Wagner had

removed his "workshop" to the ground floor and it was very probably here that the "Meistersinger" score was completed in this room on 24th October 1867,[8] which is the reason for the name "Meistersinger-room". Between the library and the dining-room on the west side a partition wall was torn down, in order to create the "Gallery", as Wagner baptized this long, narrow apartment which contained many personal mementos of the composer. The new dining-room was now considerably larger, a part of the former corridor having been added on to the older room.

A year and a half after taking possession of the new rooms Wagner sent a report, 24th February 1869, to the king describing the changes in detail. This was at the express wish of Ludwig. On the basis of this letter [9] as well as a letter from Cosima,[10] and Judith Gautier's account, we are able to reconstruct the decor and furnishings of the new ground floor. In Wagner's "green study" there were two important souvenirs on the walls: a large photographic portrait of "my royal friend" (Ludwig II), and a watercolour of Hohenschwangau, probably by Lorenzo II Quaglio, from the year 1859. It was in this castle, in November 1865, that Wagner and Ludwig celebrated what was to be the last untroubled period of their friendship, which reached a crescendo of mutual enthusiasm in this week of festivities (11th to 18th November) with which the king fêted his revered master. Wagner was housed in the castle, having a bed- and music-room at his disposal.

Books played an immensely important part in the life of the highly cultured composer, and ever since Dresden they had accompanied him on his travels before finding their final home in the Villa Wahnfried in Bayreuth. So it is not 22 surprising that in Tribschen also Wagner's main concern was his library and while here he added to it extensively. Before the winter set in, stoves and fireplaces had been installed, including the French marble mantelpiece in the salon that Cosima mentioned in her letter of 4th November 1866 to the king.

The new salon was almost exclusively decorated with oil paintings: a copy of the portrait of Wagner's stepfather, Ludwig Geyer, which the latter had himself painted; a likeness of Goethe from the hand of the Munich artist Franz v. Lenbach, inspired by an old copperplate engraving; and a copy of a Schiller-portrait by Tischbein. Besides the busts of Wagner and Ludwig II, there was in one corner an original watercolour by Genelli: "Dionysus being educated by the Muses". Wagner, who thought it a masterpiece–"I maintain it is the best thing this gifted artist has every done"–, had first come across the painting as a young man in the house of his sister, who was married to Hermann Brockhaus, and, as he wrote in the letter to Ludwig, had received from it "the first lively impressions of Greek ideals of beauty and aesthetic".

In the gallery, the middle of the long wall was occupied by the Ille watercolour of the Tannhäuser theme, a gift of the Bavarian king, and ranged on either side, were the six coloured photographs after Echter's "Rheingold", and below them objets d'art of bronze, portfolios of engraving and photographs. What little space was left on the walls was filled with other souvenirs, including an Indian Buddha figurine (Wagner contemplated a Buddha-drama, "The Victors", had sketched out the scenario, but not set it to music).

Daily life in Tribschen

In the same letter to King Ludwig, Wagner described the daily routine of life in Tribschen. Here we have space only for the main details: After cold ablutions early in the morning, a modest breakfast followed by the reading of newspapers and letters. At ten work started (at the time of writing Wagner was composing the "Siegfried"). "This allows me three undisturbed hours every day, wonderful, creative, completely satisfying mornings", wrote Wagner. At one, Jakob announced luncheon–"not very grand or artistically prepared meals, at the end of which my masters the dogs usually appear"–, then coffee in the salon, again letters and newspapers, a short midday rest "or a little work at the piano", at three, a walk with Russ and Kos, five o'clock, return to the house, a little relaxation and again composing ("if there are no letters to write"), at eight "a little supper with tea in the small salon on the first floor". Wagner mentions in this connection that the first floor is reserved for Cosima's summer visit. He was still trying to conceal his real relationship to her. In fact Cosima had finally broken with von Bülow and had joined Wagner on 16th November 1868 in Tribschen. She brought with her their two children Isolde and Eva. On 8th April 1869, von Bülow allowed Cosima the custody of the two daughters he had fathered, Daniela and Blandine, and the girls remained thenceforth in the Wagner ménage.

After the light supper with tea in the small salon of the first floor, Wagner would usually devote some time to reading–his favourites Goethe, Schiller, Shakespeare, but also Homer and Calderon–and about eleven would go off to bed in the small front room next to his study. The last part of the letter reveals how

Wagner's creative impulses had constantly to struggle with a physically week constitution: "… and now the question arises, will the night bring a sound sleep? Unfortunately this is not always the case: my stomach is in a constant state of rebellion and will remain so until I shall have undergone a thorough cure for this complaint–and so, there is sleeplessness as a result, the night becomes my enemy."

ITEMS FROM WAGNER'S HOUSEHOLD

Cosima, the daughter of Franz Liszt and the beautiful, cultured French Comtesse Marie d'Agoult, had a highly developed sensitive appreciation of the fine arts. It was very largely her taste thas was reflected in the catalogue of treasures Wagner described in his letter to the king, "which she has known how to collect for me, sometimes by the most marvellous ferreting out imaginable". Cosima had managed to obtain, for example, the Genelli watercolour Wagner prized so greatly. She persuaded his sister to part with it, and had the pleasure of presenting it to Wagner. And she, too, chose the picture-frames, or ordered them to be made according to her specific requirements, in both cases showing the "most imaginative sensibility" in her choice. By her own admission: "I like pictures better than books"[13], she confirmed where her artistic feelings lay. So it seemed an obvious course to put such pictures into the museum that would convey something of the atmosphere as it was in Tribschen in Wagner's time there. For very little has remained of the original objects of that period.

The most valuable and outstanding object is certainly the Erard grand piano, loaned by Winifred Wagner and her children. A gift from the widow of the Parisian pianomaker Pierre Erard, the piano arrived in Wagner's "place of exile" in Zurich-Enge on 3rd May 1858. Wagner used the instrument in Venice and in 1859 in Lucerne during the five months of his stay at the hotel "Schweizerhof", then took it with him to Paris, Vienna and Munich, Tribschen and Bayreuth. The music of the second and third acts of "Tristan" was first heard on this piano. It now stands, after the renovation of the museum, in its original place in the salon. Of the furniture, that by the nature of things is particularly susceptible to the ravages of time, there are only an occasional table with painted top, the armchair in which Wagner was often photographed, and a footstool. Then the two original petroleum lamps of alabaster and bronze. A gift from Ludwig II is the splendid goblet of Bohemian glass, made circa 1830. The domed lid of this goblet is richly engraved: deer and roebuck under high trees in a meadow landscape with a forest background. Among the precious requisites that recall the period, is the golden Geneva watch with engraved date, that Richard Wagner presented to his godchild, Jakob Wilhelm Stocker, on 6th June 1869, to commemorate the birth of his own son, Siegfried.

Of the clothes Wagner had worn in Tribschen, there are a silk shirt with lace frills, laundry-marked R.W.4, and a dark brown velvet jacket, both presents from the Zurich artist Jean Lehmann, the house jacket owned by Wagner's friend, the merchant Sorokoumow, whose nephew Trifon Trapesnikoff, Dornach, handed it on to Hans Reinhart in Winterthur who presented it and the velvet beret to the museum. The collection has been added to: the capote hat that Cosima wore in Tribschen. Apropos of silk and velvet: Wagner liked to surround himself with the luxuries of life, and his debts and perpetual money shortage were in no small measure due to his tailor's and milliner's bills.[14] But there is also another explanation for his love of silks and satins: he could not bear wool and cotton next to his skin, suffering all his life from an allergy; medical treatment frequently taken, without lasting results. A whip, gift of the house of Am Rhyn (which family also donated the occasional table), brings to mind the dog-lover Wagner, who in Tribschen had the companionship of the New-foundlander Russ as well as Cosima's fox ter-rier Kos; Russ followed his master to Bay-reuth, and lies buried next to him in the garden of the Villa Wahnfried.[15]

A plaster cast of Wagner's right hand, donated by Frau S. Bergman, Oberursel, and Wagner's death-mask produce in the spectator all those feelings before the face of human mortality that are expressed in respectful silence. For a long time there was considerable doubt as to whether this was the original death-mask. The facts are as follows: The previous owner of the mask now exhibited in Tribschen was the artist and writer L. Brosch, Venice. His father had obtained the death-mask from the sculptor Augusto Benvenuti (8.1.1838–7.2.1899) who had made it. Benvenuti, who lived near the Vendramin Palace where Wagner died on 13th February 1883, had made *several* death-masks, unknown to the family. So it cannot be said with certainty which one was the "first".

Four engravings, that hung in Wagner's study, are reminders of the musical gods the compo-ser honoured: Christoph Willibald Gluck, Joseph Haydn, Ludwig van Beethoven and Wolfgang Amadeus Mozart.

Photographs, busts and portraits of Wagner
Of the many original photographs, lithographic portraits and busts of Wagner, only the most important are mentioned here. In the former study three large blow-up photographs domi-nate the scene: the one shows Richard Wagner in his favourite armchair, a portrait made in 1867; the second is, in a sense, the official wed-ding photograph of Richard Wagner and Cosima, although it was taken two years after the event, in Vienna; the third is of Wagner with the newly born Eva in his arms (she was born 17th February 1867 in Tribschen) and his dog Russ at his feet. The original photograph taken in 1867, with a handwritten dedication of the master, is one of the more valuable docu-ments left to the museum by Eva Chamberlain. The pencil sketch, executed on squared paper from a notebook, is by the painter Paul von Joukowsky and shows Wagner in a character-istic pose, reading aloud from la Motte-Fou-qué's "Undine" on his last evening, the 12th February 1883. Liszt, Hermann Levi, Joukow-sky were probably his last visitors... An orig-inal lithograph after the watercolour by Cle-mentine Stockar-Escher of Zurich, depicting Wagner in Zurich in 1853, carries an autograph dedication to his concert-master in that town, Wilhelm Heisterhagen. In one corner of the li-brary stands the bronze bust by Caspar Zum-busch. The portrait in oils of Wagner hanging in the salon is a copy of the fine painting by Franz von Lenbach (1836–1904) now in Bay-reuth (the copy was made by Margarete von Bodecker). Lenbach was a talented and fashionable portrait painter of the time, whose sitters included most of those with rank and name in Central Europe. Of greater signifi-cance from the artistic point of view is the Re-noir lithograph of Wagner. It differs slightly

from the oil painting by the great French impressionist (which is exhibited here in reproduction) and is a gift to the museum by the Lucerne art collector Siegfried Rosengart, who was a friend of Picasso. The glory of the collection however is the original oil painting, "Richard Wagner in his Bayreuth home". This impressive work (145 × 170 cm) by Wilhelm Beckmann (1852–1942), was painted in 1882, the year of the "Parsifal" premiere and shows Wagner, Franz Liszt and Cosima together with Baron Hans Paul von Wolzogen (1848–1938), editor and publisher of the «Bayreuther Blätter», who was a major figure in the Villa Wahnfried circle. Beckmann's conversation piece, that is reproduced in practically every pictorial biography of Wagner, was discovered in a Scottish castle by the Lucerne art expert Paul Fischer, who afterwards offered it for sale to the city of Lucerne. The purchase sum of Sfr. 12,000 was raised, largely by private donors, and the painting now hangs in the salon of Tribschen.

A number of other paintings deal with themes from the Wagnerian music dramas, attempting to visualize the content and mood. Hans Thoma (1839–1924), commissioned by Cosima, produced in 1890 a pictorial "Ring"-cycle: four watercolours, "The Rhine Daughters", "Siegfried in the Forest", "The Three Norns" and "The armed Brünnhilde". The last-named of these, different in format from the others, came into the possession of the museum: Daniela Thode von Bülow bequeathed it in her testament in gratitude for the holidays she had been enabled to spend in Tribschen. Motives of the "Ring" tetralogy, that was almost half completed in Tribschen, appear also in "Wotan's Farewell" and "Siegfried" ("Forest Webs") by Ferdinand Leeke (1859–1931). Also by Leeke is the painting that touches on the theme of Wagner's last work: "Parsifal before the Castle of the Grail".

The triptych by Franz Stassen (1869–1949), in pure Art Nouveau, depicts key scenes from Wagner's most passionate opera, "Tristan and Isolde", of which the third act was composed in the hotel "Schweizerhof" in Lucerne. In the central panel, Tristan and Isolde are shown as lovers, to the right is Isolde with the love potion, and the left one depicts the mortally wounded Tristan. (Actually there are five scenes in all, the reverse of the two side panels being painted also.)

"Politically dangerous individual No. 652"

The task the Wagner Museum in Tribschen must set itself is that main one of documenting the Swiss years and particularly the period of active composition, and the major part of the exhibited material emphasizes this aspect. Still there are one or two documents that bear witness to decisive moments in Wagner's earlier life and these deserve to be mentioned. Among the more recent acquisitions, a gift from two ladies in France is the score of a pianoforte and song arrangement from the Donizetti opera "La Favorite", "arrangée par R.W." of the year 1841. This is one of the "pot-boilers" Wagner was forced to produce in his Paris period–the hunger years–in order to survive. Another newly obtained document is the warrant issued against the young, revolutionary Richard Wagner: Actually it is a likeness of Wagner in "Eberhard's Police Gazette" of 11th June 1853, and a former owner had copied out the warrant, that had appeared in the Police Gazette, onto the back of it: "Politically dangerous individual No. 652, Wagner Richard, former Kapellmeister in Dresden, one of the most brilliant partisans of the revolutionary party, a warrant for whose arrest has been issued because of his participation in the revolution in Dresden May 1849, intends, according to our information, to return from Zurich to Germany. A likeness of Wagner is attached herewith, to facilitate the apprehending of the same who is to be arrested on entering the country and delivered over to the Crown Court of Justice in Dresden."

Minna–Mathilde–Cosima

There is impressive documentation and pictorial material in the Wagner Museum at Tribschen about the three women who played a major rôle in the composer's life. Let us begin with *Minna née Planer* (1809–1866), Richard Wagner's first wife, who had accompanied him from Dresden to Switzerland and remained true to her vows to stand by him in times of distress and need. The picture of the actress Minna Planer with the little dog Peps is the reproduction of a watercolour by the Zurich artist Clementine Stockar-Escher, of 1853. An interesting document is the dedicatory poem on the occasion of the wedding of Minna Planer to Richard Wagner on 24th November 1836 in Königsberg, a gift of the Basel Wagnerite Adolf Zinsstag. The dithyrambic rhythm of the poem is somewhat surprising. Wagner was deeply in debt, but that had not prevented him having this poem, partly printed on silk, reproduced in sufficient numbers to be handed out to the wedding guests.

Mathilde Wesendonck (1828–1902) "was, after Schopenhauer, the second reason for Wagner's mood to find expression in the ecstatic love and death drama of Tristan and Isolde".[16] It is difficult to decide what one should more ad-

mire, the marble bust by. L. Keiser, Zurich, done in the year 1860, or the wonderful portrait in pastels by Ernst Benedikt Kietz that shows Wagner's Zurich woman friend with her little son, Guido (who died young), taken in December 1856. The charcoal drawing by the same artist is a preliminary sketch for the pastel portrait and was presented to the museum by Friedrich Frey-Fürst. The five poems written by Mathilde Wesendonck, "Der Engel" (The Angel), "Stehe still" (Stand still), "Im Treibhaus" (In the Conservatory), "Schmerzen" (Pain) and "Träume" (Dreams), set to music by Richard Wagner for solo voice and piano, are here in the first editions, separately bound, from the years 1857–1858. In addition the museum received a facsimile-copy of the Wesendonck songs in 1969.

Cosima Liszt (1837–1930) is immortalized in two Lenbach portraits: while the one, like that of Richard Wagner, is a copy (the original was painted in 1879), the pastel portrait is a genuine Lenbach, a profile view in delicate grey and brown tones.[17] The beautiful marble bust of Cosima by Gustav Kietz (1824–1908) is a copy of the one in the Villa Wahnfried in Bayreuth. The young sculptor Gustav Kietz was a friend of Wagner, who often used to receive him in his Dresden apartment, when he was still married to Minna.

Malwida von Meysenbug

Together with the portraits of Hans von Bülow and Malwida von Meysenbug, there are thus three original Lenbach works in the Wagner museum. Malwida von Meysenbug (1816–1903), the clever and witty writer ("Memoirs of an Idealist"), was an enthusiastic disciple and belonged to the intimate circle of friends in

Tribschen. So she, with Hans Richter, was a witness at the wedding of Wagner and Cosima on 25th August 1870 in Lucerne.[18] As early as 1855 she had first come in contact with the master, had lived through the great "Tannhäuser"-scandal in Paris in 1861, and from 1870 on she was a constant visitor in the Wagner household, settling down in Bayreuth in 1873. Wagner always regarded her as one of the family, the friend of Cosima and the educator of his children. The nine (original) letters here which he had written to her, give proof of the very close personal relationship that existed: Of the 53 letters of Richard Wagner which the museum possesses 45 are original ones, of which 31 belong to the Tribschen period (1866–1872). Six are to Col. Am Rhyn, the owner of the house, three to Professor Riedl, concertmaster in Leipzig, two each to Vreneli, the Lucerne artist Zelger, the Lucerne bookseller Prell, E.W. Fritzsch, Leipzig publisher, one each to Jos. Hellmesberger, Vienna, Dr. Ferd. Leutner, Vienna, Hans Richter, Vienna, and to Friedrich Nietzsche.

The letters of Wagner to Malwida von Meysenbug are supplemented by the letters of Malwida to her foster-daughter Olga Herzen, published by Berta Schleicher under the title "Im Anfang war die Liebe" (In the Beginning was Love) and dedicated to the Richard Wagner Museum in Tribschen.

Hans Richter (1843–1916) belonged to the inner circle of friends in Tribschen, and a number of exhibits testify to his presence there: a copy of a photograph (gift from the Richard Wagner Archives, Bayreuth) shows him during the Tribschen period; a lithograph of 1893, signed by him (a gift of the Vienna Academic Association); among the more important documents are the sketches of the first act of the "Meistersinger" and the handwritten copy of the full score of "Siegfried", that Hans Richter completed in Tribschen (a present from Hans Paul Baron von Wolzogen, Bayreuth). And with this one comes to the principle occupation of Richter in Tribschen: the young Viennese hornplayer and concertmaster, recommended to Wagner by the Vienna concertmasters Heinrich Esser and Joseph Hellmesberger, was both secretary and copyst. He was a guest of the house for 23 months, occupying the room on the second floor overlooking the lake, that was later to be Friedrich Nietzsche's room. During this period, from 30th October 1866 until 1st December 1867 he made a fair copy of the score of the "Meistersinger". On 26th June 1870, Richter was once more in Tribschen and made a fair copy of the complete "Siegfried" between then and the middle of April 1871. During his stay with the Wagner family he also made fair copies of a number of other works by Wagner: "Beethoven", "About Opera", "Concerning the Performance of the Music Drama 'The Ring of the Nibelungs' ".[20] But Richter was also active as a musician, being not only a horn player but a violinist and viola player as well. And in Tribschen he learnt the trumpet, the instrument he played at the first performance of the "Siegfried Idyll" on Christmas Day 1870. And, together with the Zurich musicians Oskar Kahl, Hermann Ruhoff and Georg Rauchenecker, he created that "Tribschen Quartet" which, in the Beethoven year, from October 1870 to March 1871 with regular chamber music concerts every Sunday in Tribschen, gave performances of all the Beethoven quartets.[21] Later Hans Richter conducted the first complete performance of the "Ring" in Bayreuth Festival Hall, 1876.

Civic documents

After this brief digression we return again to things more immediate, to the family circle and the local connections, of which the Tribschen museum provides a great deal of evidence. For Wagner, his residence here meant more than the feelings of stability and permanency which it undoubtedly gave: it was also the time of his being established as an "established" citizen. To these civic documents belong the marriage certificate of Richard Wagner with Cosima, formerly von Bülow, in the marriage register of the Lucerne Protestant parish (photocopied for the Wagner Museum, with the kind permission of the church authorities); the wedding announcement printed by the Lucerne lithographers Eglin Bros., whom Wagner knew personally; the entry of Siegfried's birth in the Register of Births of the Lucerne Protestant parish (photographic reproduction); the menu on the occasion of the dinner celebrating Siegfried Wagner's baptism, 4th September 1870; Richard Wagner's handwritten letter of 25th August 1871 to Pastor Heinrich Tschudi in Lucerne, who had officiated at both the wedding and the baptism, announcing the payment of a donation to the community of the Reformed Church, "in grateful remembrance of the blessed act of my marriage with my dear wife, which ceremony you performed with so much sympathy a year ago today"; the baptismal certificate of Eva, born 17th February 1867 in Tribschen, and, like Siegfried later, baptized in the church of St. Matthew Lucerne, where the entry in the register gives her name as Eva Maria *von Bülow* (Wagner's liaison with Cosima, who had already borne him a daughter, Isolde, on 10th April 1865, was then still kept secret).

Two letters testify to the friendly relationship with the painter Franz Zelger, who had his studio in the garden of the hotel "Schweizerhof", where Wagner used to visit him: in the letter of 19th May 1868, shown together with the envelope carrying the monogram R.W., Wagner thanks him for the present of a painting, and in the letter of 7th August 1868, Wagner invites Zelger and his wife to luncheon at Tribschen. Further there is a photograph of Richard Wagner with a dedication in his own hand "To Prof. Zelger", and the textbook of the "Meistersinger" containing a dedication from Wagner to Zelger.

Odyssey of a lease

Mementos and documents are not only signposts along the road of an artist's career, sometimes they have their own story to tell. So it is, for example, with the original lease exhibited in the museum. This contract, drawn up between Wagner and Lt.-Col. Walter Ludwig Am Rhyn on 7th April 1866 committed Wagner to leasing the Tribschen house and property for one year at a rental of three thousand franks. On 26th June 1963, during the celebrations in connection with the 150th anniversary of Wagner's birth, this document, a paper of lightish brown colour, was stolen from the Tribschen museum by some person unknown. For several years its whereabouts was a mystery. Then, in 1969, the Helmhaus in Zurich presented an exhibition of music manuscripts and among the items on show were the original score of the "Siegfried Idyll"–and the lease. It did not take Dr. Robert Kaufmann, secretary to Lucerne's mayor and onetime custodian of the Tribschen museum, very long to discover that this lease was identical with the one stolen from the museum in 1963. Further investigation revealed that it had been offered for sale at a public auction held in the New York auction house of Charles Hamilton in May 1964 and had been bought–quite legally–by a Dr. R.F. Kallir of New York. Dr. Kallir spontaneously offered the document to Lucerne as a gift, and the lease came back to its original home after an odyssey that had taken it to New York and Zurich.[22]

"Vreneli"

Verena Stocker-Weidmann (1832–1906) of Embrach in the canton of Zurich, held a special position in the Wagner household in Tribschen. She is represented in the museum by a photograph taken of an older picture and an original letter to Bertha Goldwag in Vienna (dated Tribschen, 21st March 1869). She is the "Vreneli" of all the Wagner biographies, which use the name he familiarly gave her. She had come into his service for the first time in 1859, an intelligent, dedicated young woman, whose care for her master during his stay at the "Schweizerhof" that year, where he completed the "Tristan", prompted him to ask her to continue in his service when he moved to Munich. In Munich as in Tribschen, and in-between in the country-house "Les Artichauts" near Geneva, Vreneli was in charge of the household. The dog Russ so frequently mentioned was a present from Vrenely to Wagner; she had bought it with money she had saved. Her husband, the loyal, diligent Jakob Stocker, was accepted by Vreneli only on the condition that he too would become a servant at Tribschen. When the final move to Bayreuth came, however, Vreneli quitted the Wagner's service. But Wagner always thought of her with the utmost gratitude and many letters testify to the affectionate feelings he and Cosima felt for their "Vreneli". A letter of Wagner, dated 22nd December 1874, from Bayreuth, begins with the words: "Dear Vreneli, So I shall always call you, in memory of the times when you and your good Jakob vouchsafed me so much loyalty and love." And the 69-year old Wagner, writing barely two months before his death, from the Palazzo Vendramin in Venice, Canal Grande, on 27th December 1882, to Frau Verena Stocker, im Moos near Lucerne, Svizzera: "My good, dear Vreneli, Are we still alive?–Now we certainly want to convince ourselves of that next spring, when about May in any case we return over the Gotthard and then in Lucerne we are going to look you up." That was not to be, however. Richard Wagner died in the palazzo in Venice on 13th February 1883. In his letter to Vreneli he had told her that he had instructed his banker to send her the scholarship money for his godson (Wilhelm, the Stocker's son, whom he had presented with a gold watch on 6th June 1869).[23]

From the Tribschen period there are two original letters that Wagner wrote to Vreneli Stocker from Munich (1867 and 1868), while the two original letters from Cosima to Vreneli were written long after Wagner's death, on 22nd May 1897 and 7th June 1897–testimony of the enduring nature of the relationship between the former housekeeper and the Wagner family that continued long after the direct contact was over.

First editions

Besides a few shorter original manuscripts of Richard Wagner (recommendation of the String Quartet, founded in Zurich 1853, the poem "An dich" (To Thee) for Cosima, Starnberg, 1st October 1864, the poem to Ludwig II, "Am Abgrund steh' ich" (I stand on the Precipice), Hochkopf, 12th August 1865, poem to

Ludwig II, "on 25.8.1868", with verse dedication by Cosima Wagner) there are numerous first editions in Tribschen testifying to the literary activity of Wagner during his residence there. "On Conducting" was written in the autumn of 1869 and published in December of the same year (although dated 1870) in Leipzig. "German Art and German Politics" was published in a definitive edition by J.J. Weber. "Beethoven" was written in August and September 1870 in Tribschen and published in November 1870 by E.W. Fritzsch in Leipzig. "On the Nature of Opera" was a lecture produced by Wagner in the spring of 1871 in Tribschen and read by him to the Royal Academy of Arts in Berlin on 28th April of the same year. The essay takes up the thread of the concepts given in "Opera and Drama" and was printed in Leipzig in 1871. "Opera and Drama" written in Zurich in the winter of 1850/51, was produced in a revised edition by Wagner, the foreword bearing the date: Tribschen, near Lucerne, 28th April 1868. "Judaism in Music" is also a new edition of the article that first appeared in Franz Brendel's "New Music Journal" in 1850. It is dedicated to Frau Marie Muchanoff (1823–1874), who had paid Tribschen a visit a short time before. The epilogue is dated: Tribschen near Lucerne, New Year 1869, and the revised edition appeared in February in Leipzig. "Concerning the Performance of the Musical Drama 'The Ring of the Nibelungen'" was written in Tribschen at the beginning of April 1871. It is both a notice of intentions and invitation to the friends of his art and was published in Leipzig in 1871. Among the other first editions are "On actors and singers", Leipzig 1872, and "Report to the German Wagner Association", Leipzig 1872. From the pre-Tribschen period are "The Nibelungen-Saga and World History", completed in Zurich 1849, and published in Leipzig 1850; "Music of the Future", published Leipzig 1861. In the post-Tribschen period come "On Religion and Art" (1881) and "Jesus of Nazareth" (1887), a poetic creation of Richard Wagner that had been written as far back as 1848, however. Wagner had had the Tribschen writings bound, with the titles in gold on the cover, and had made a gift of them to his wife.

Friedrich Nietzsche

Undoubtedly the most illustrious personality to join the Wagnerite circle was Friedrich Nietzsche (1844–1900). It is therefore fitting and just that there should be a separate display cabinet reserved for memorials of the philosopher who visited Wagner 23 times on the "Isle of the Blest", as Nietzsche christened the Tribschen peninsula. The so-called Nietzsche Cabinet, in which documents relating to the friendship between Wagner and Ludwig II are also exhibited, contains among other things: the death-mask in bronze, photographs of the young (Pforta 1864) and the older Nietzsche, as well as the two most significant documents, which pinpoint the beginning and the end of this relationship between these two intellects, a relationship whose precise nature has never been fully explained to this day: the first edition of the "Birth of Tragedy out of the Spirit of Music", Leipzig 1872, which, not only written under the strong influence of Wagnerian art, also bore the stamp of Wagner's dominating personality; and the first edition of the brief essay, "The Wagner Case: A musician's problem", Leipzig 1888, written in Turin in the spring of that year.

The collection of letters in the Tribschen museum contains six letters of Friedrich

Nietzsche, including an original one in which the disparity between the poet-philosopher and the composer is very clearly expressed. It was written to Fräulein Mathilde Maier and bears the postmark, Basel, 18th July 1878. It begins with the words: "... it can't be helped: I have to hurt all my friends–precisely because I speak out at last, which helps me out of my own distress. That metaphysical befogging of all that is true and simple, the struggle with that reason which sees in all and everything the miraculous and the monstrous added to this, a truly baroque art of hypertension and glorification of excess–I mean Wagner's art–these two things made me more and more ill and nearly robbed me of my good temperament and my talent."

Nietzsche's happier days as a young man–he was 24 when he met Wagner for the first time–on the "Isle of the Blest", are reflected in the following passage from his letter to Erwin Rhode, written 3rd September 1869: "Another thing, I also have my Italy, like you, the difference being this saving grace comes to me only on Saturdays and Sundays. It is called Tribschen and I am already quite at home in the place. Recently I was there four times in a row, moreover every week a letter flies in the same direction. Dearest friend, I cannot put in words what I learn and observe there, hear and understand. Schopenhauer and Goethe, Aeschylus and Pindar still live, believe me."

Autographs, manuscripts and facsimiles
"Some of the most important opera acts of the century were created on this idyllic peninsula", said Gregor-Dellin in his summing-up of Wagner's achievements during the six years in Tribschen. They began with the "Meistersinger von Nürnberg" and ended with the "Göt-terdämmerung" (The Twilight of the Gods), the keystone of the great "Ring" tetralogy. We have Cosima's statement: "The 'Meistersinger' is wholly a Tribschen work" and about the "Twilight of the Gods" she said: "In Tribschen I witnessed the 'Götterdämmerung' growing up; every bar created I felt as my own, and I followed with passionate devotion the evolution of this tremendous work."

What documents of these productive years are exhibited in the museum? The original scores of the "Meistersinger", "Siegfried", "Göt-terdämmerung" and "Tristan" are in Bayreuth. But the Wagner Museum has nevertheless a few very interesting individual pieces and facsimiles of the original scores of the "Meistersinger", "Tristan and Isolde" and "Siegfried". There is also a pianoforte arrangement, 1871, by Karl Klindworth of the "Siegfried" with an original dedication from the master to the Wesendonck family in Zurich. The oldest source of the "Meistersinger" story is the Nuremberg Chronicle of Johann Christophorus Wagenseil, with an appendix, "A report on the sweet art of the master singers", dated 1697 (Altorf near Nuremberg). A copy is exhibited in the museum. Wagner took from it not only the names of the masters, the rules of the contest, ect., but the musical motif of his opera was adapted from the first seven notes of the "long tones" of Heinrich Mügling given in the account.

At the end of October 1869 Richard Wagner had observed the Lucerne Fire Brigade in action and he wrote and composed a short song for male voices in their honour (8th November 1869): "Loyalty be our garb/Love the banner/Energy our word/And God our greatest shield." A printed copy is displayed in the museum, the actual manuscript is unfortunately missing (Wagner dedicated the same motto, however, to the German fire-fighters as well). On the other hand, there is an original Wagner manuscript in the archives of the Lucerne School of Music: it is his arrangement of the "Homage March" (1864) which the Lucerne Brass Band performed under his windows on 22nd May 1870, to mark the occasion of his 57th birthday. Another item the Tribschen museum displays is the piano arrangement by Karl Tausig of the "Emperor March" which Wagner composed in Tribschen in January/February 1871 to celebrate the founding of the Second German Empire.

An original music manuscript is the complete orchestral score of the "Cobbler's Song" from the "Meistersinger", with a large photographic portrait of the author and a dedication in his own hand to "His dear Mastersinger and good friend Betz. With great joy and in fond memory of the admirable cobbling. Tribschen near Lucerne, July 1868, Richard Wagner." The singer Franz Betz, by taking the place of the indisposed singer Beck as the first "Hans Sachs", made it possible to hold the premiere of the opera on 21st June 1868 in the Munich Royal and National Theatre as arranged. Linked with these items are the generously donated sketches of the first act of the "Meistersinger" with notes written to Cosima as well as two bars from the score of the "Meistersinger" (oboe, clarinet and horn parts to Kotner's "Leges Tabulaturae", original score, page 113).

Examples of Wagner's poesy are the first draft of the poem "The young Siegfried", which was purchased 1951, exactly one hundred years after it was written, and the transcript of the "Dutchman" manuscripts with the old names (Donald instead of Daland, Georg instead of Erik). "The young Siegfried", signed and dated Zurich, 24th June 1851, 12 noon, is the germ cell from which the mighty tetralogy of the "Ring of the Nibelungs" grew. In 1962 the museum acquired a facsimile copy of the text of the "Ring" based on the original edition limited to fifty copies published in Zurich in 1853. An original manuscript is the composition sketch of part of Waltraut's rôle from the first act of the "Twilight of the Gods" (in ink), a gift to the museum from Frau Sophie Bergmann, Oberursel.

The Wagner Museum's greatest treasure is the original score of the "Siegfried Idyll" with the dedicatory poem. Wagner had given the manuscript to Hans Richter as a gift. With the imminent realization of the Wagner museum project in mind, Richter's heirs offered the original score of the "Siegfried Idyll" for sale to Lucerne in 1932. The price was Sfr. 27,000. At that time the economic crisis weighed heavily on the public sector and private persons and institutions were called upon to help. A part of the sum was met personally by the Basel goldsmith and music lover *Adolf Zinstag-Preiswerk*. The rest, still amounting to Sfr. 21,230, was paid by the "Luzerner Stiftung für Suchende" (Lucerne Cultural Aid Foundation). As the foundation considered its acquisition of the manuscript to come under the heading, literary activities, the composition came into the possession of the city library, which passed it on to the Wagner museum as a loan exhibit. During the making of the film about Richard Wagner in 1982, the original score was facsimiled. Since then only the facsimile is displayed–the same is true, incidentally, for the manuscript "The young Siegfried"– in order to preserve the original in good condition. It is now kept in the safe. (Bibliography: see version in German.)

TRIBSCHEN:
A GENERAL GUIDE TO THE MAIN
EXHIBITS

Room 1
(formerly Richard Wagner's bedroom):
Lithographs of Richard Wagner, Hans Richter and Franz Liszt; coloured lithograph of Hotel Schweizerhof, circa 1860; coloured lithograph of Tribschen, circa 1828; charcoal drawing by Ernst Benedikt Rietz of Mathilde Wesendonck with her young son Guido, 1856; the Wagner family-tree with photographs of his descendants.

Room 2
(formerly Wagner's "Green Study", also known as the "Meistersinger" room):
The glass display cabinet contains the sole surviving letter written by Wagner's stepfather; documents of Wagner's first wife, Minna Planer; "The Young Siegfried" manuscript, 1851, in the author's own hand; likeness of Cosima and Richard Wagner (among others a lithograph from the year 1853); three blow-ups of Wagner photos (Wagner in his armchair, Tribschen, 1867; with Eva and the Newfoundland dog Russ, Tribschen, 1867; with Cosima in Vienna, 1872); portraits of Cosima's parents and her brother and sister, of Verena Stocker-Weidmann (1832–1906) and Jakob Stocker (1827–1909) as well as of Franz Zelger and Pastor J.H. Tschudi; Richard Wagner's and Cosima's marriage announcement, the birth certificates of the children Eva and Siegfried; the lease and original letters to the owner of Tribschen, Col. Am Rhyn; warrant with likeness of Wagner; plaster cast of Wagner's right hand; the short male chorus for the Lucerne Fire Brigade, 1869; letters to Franz Liszt, Hans Richter, Malwida von Meysenbug, Verena Stocker-Weidmann and others.

Among other items of interest are the original armchair in which Wagner often had himself portrayed, the whip for the Newfoundlander Russ and–in a separate showcase–some of Wagner's favourite clothes, Cosima's capote hat, and the sole original letter from Verena Stocker-Weidmann (to Wagner's tailoress in Vienna, Bertha Goldwag).

Room 3
(formerly the salon, with the original fireplace):
Oil portraits of Richard and Cosima Wagner (copies of the paintings by Franz von Lenbach); original painting of Hans von Bülow and original pastel portraits of Cosima and Malwida von Meysenbug by Franz von Lenbach; original pastel portrait of Mathilde Wesendonck with her son Guido by Ernst Ben-

edikt Kietz; original pencil drawing of Emilie Heims by Clementine Stockar-Escher; original painting "Richard Wagner in his Bayreuth home" by Wilhelm Beckmann; occasional table with painted top and two petroleum lamps from Wagner's household; the Erard grand piano; four steel engravings that decorated Wagner's study (Gluck, Haydn, Mozart, Beethoven); the original score of the "Siegfried Idyll" with dedicatory poem; facsimile edition of the original scores of the "Meistersinger", "Siegfried" and "Tristan and Isolde"; the Nuremberg Chronicle of Johann Christophorus Wagenseil, 1697; first editions of literary works written in Tribschen; Wagner's death-mask.

Room 4
(formerly the gallery or library):
Busts of Richard Wagner, Cosima Wagner and Mathilde Wesendonck; on the walls pictures of visitors and guests in Tribschen; in the showcase mementos of Wagner's patron and disciple, Ludwig II of Bavaria and of his friend Friedrich Nietzsche (death-mask, first editions of "The Birth of Tragedy" and "The Problem of Wagner"); bookcases with Wagner literature.

Room 5
(the former dining-room):
Theatre tickets and illustrations of opera houses in which Wagner's works were given their premier performances; decor and stage settings in Bayreuth ("Parsifal") and photographs (mostly autographed) of the principle male and female soloists of the Wagner operas; the original orchestral score of the "Cobbler's Song" from the "Meistersinger"; a fair copy of the "Dutchman" manuscript with the old names; the original lithograph portrait of Wagner by Auguste Renoir; Franz Stassen's triptych "Tristan and Isolde"; four watercolours by Hans Thoma, illustrating themes out of the "Ring"; Richard Wagner's Life and Works 1813–1834 (an incomplete biography based on original letters and documents of the Burrell Collection, Philadelphia, published in 1898 by Mrs. Mary Burrell, large folio, numbered copy, No 67).

NOTES

[1] Tribschener Blätter Nr. 2, Mai 1957.

[2] Max Fehr: Richard Wagners Schweizer Zeit, Band 2, Aarau 1953, Seite 227.

[3] Robert Kaufmann: Das Richard-Wagner-Museum in Tribschen, Schriftenreihe Luzern im Wandel der Zeiten, Heft 10, Luzern 1962, Seite 14.

[4] Luzerner Neueste Nachrichten Nr. 194, 13. August 1938, Seite 15, «Bei Richard Wagner und Cosima».

[5] Max Fehr: Richard Wagners Schweizer Zeit, Band 2, Seite 224 ff.

[6] Die Kunstdenkmäler des Kantons Luzern, Band 3, Die Stadt Luzern, 2. Teil, Basel 1954, Seite 268.

[7] Max Fehr: Richard Wagners Schweizer Zeit, Seite 227, nach Du Moulin: Cosima Wagner, Band 1, Seite 287.

[8] Max Fehr: Richard Wagners Schweizer Zeit, Band 2, Seite 258.

[9] Richard Wagner: Mein Leben, Band 2, München 1963/69, Seite 773.

[10] Cosimas Brief an den König, datiert vom 4. November 1866.

[11] Judith Gautier: Le troisième Rang du Collier, Seiten 21, 22, 39, 54, 92, 113.

[12] Martin Gregor-Dellin: Richard Wagner, eine Biographie in Bildern, München 1982, Seite 137.

[13] Robert Kaufmann: Das Richard-Wagner-Museum in Tribschen, Seite 17.

[14] Erich Kuby: «Die Welt ist mir schuldig, was ich brauche», in Zeit-Magazin Nr. 6, Februar 1983.

[15] Vgl. dazu Henri Perrier: Les chiens de Wagner, Lyon 1982.

[16] Martin Gregor-Dellin: Richard Wagner, eine Biographie in Bildern, München 1982, Seite 100.

[17] Luzerner Neueste Nachrichten Nr. 184, 4. August 1939.

[18] Tribschener Blätter Nr. 10, Mai 1961.

[19] Die Briefe im Tribschener Museum sind von Adolf Zinsstag gesammelt und chronologisch geordnet 1961 unter dem Titel «Die Briefsammlungen des Richard-Wagner-Museums in Tribschen bei Luzern» herausgegeben worden.

[20] Max Fehr: Richard Wagners Schweizer Zeit, Band 2, Seite 309.

[21] Anton Schmid, Das Richard-Wagner-Museum in Tribschen, 2. Auflage, Luzern 1938.

[22] Luzerner Neueste Nachrichten in Tribschener Blätter Nr. 26, Dezember 1969.

[23] Richard Wagner an Vreneli, e.k. Neue Zürcher Zeitung, 24. Mai 1934.

1

1   *Former salon in Richard Wagner's home, after restoration of the museum in 1983. In the foreground is the Erard grand piano, in the background the fireplace that Wagner had installed*

2   *Schweizerhofquai, the hotels "Schweizerhof" and "Englischer Hof", with the first steamship and the collegiate church of St. Leodegar (circa 1870). Coloured engraving*

3   *Hans Guido Freiherr von Bülow (1830–1894). Original portrait in oils by Franz von Lenbach, Munich (1880)*

4   *Malwida von Meysenbug (1816–1903). Witness at the marriage ceremony in Lucerne 1870 and Siegfried's godmother. Original pastel by Franz von Lenbach, Munich (1872)*

Page 41
Franz Stassen (1869–1949), painter, graphic artist, stage designer: Triptych "Tristan and Isolde", exterior of grand piano (circa 1916)

2

3

4

Ferdinand Leeke (1859–1931), "Waldweben" ("Tanglewood"). Original oil painting (1920)

Page 45
Richard Wagner at 40, signed lithograph after the watercolour by Clementine Stockar-Escher, Zurich 1853

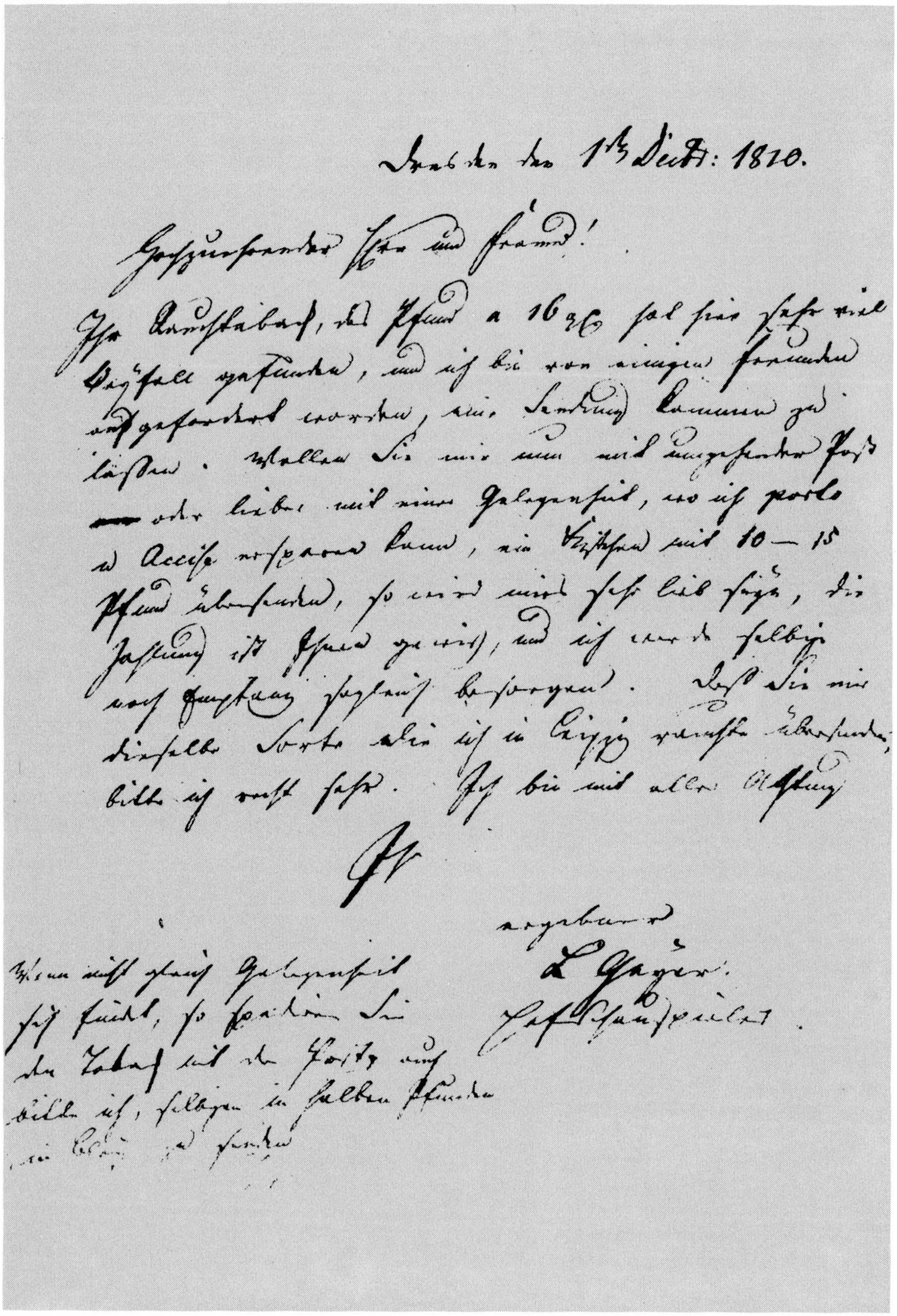

Dresden den 1ten Decb: 1810.

Hochzuverehrender Herr und Freund!

Ihr Rauchtabak, das Pfund a 16 gr hat hier sehr viel Beifall gefunden, und ich bin von einigen Freunden aufgefordert worden, eine Sendung kommen zu lassen. Wollen Sie mir nun mit umgehender Post — oder lieber mit einer Gelegenheit, wo ich porto u. Accise ersparen kann, ein Kistchen mit 10 — 15 Pfund übersenden, so wird mir sehr lieb seyn, die Zahlung ist Ihnen gewiss, und ich werde selbige nach Empfang sogleich besorgen. Daß Sie mir dieselbe Sorte aber ich in Leipzig rauchte übersenden, bitte ich recht sehr. Ich bin mit aller Achtung

Ihr

ergebener

L. Geyer.

Hofschauspieler.

Wenn sich keine Gelegenheit sich findet, so schicken Sie den Tabak mit der Post und bitte ich, selbigen in halben Pfunden [illegible] zu packen

1

1 Ludwig Geyer (1779–1821). Richard Wagner's stepfather: Letter to the merchant Schrader, Leipzig, 1st December 1810

2 Richard Wagner's birthplace, on the Brühl ("marsh"), Leipzig, torn down in 1886 (photograph)

3 Johanna Rosine Wagner, née Pätz (1774–1848), the composer's mother, portrait by Ludwig Geyer, circa 1818 (reproduction)

4 Ludwig Geyer (1779–1821). Self-portrait (circa 1818). Reproduction

2

3

4

An Fräulein

Minna Planer

bei ihrem

Vermählungs-Feste

mit dem

Musikdirector Herrn

Richard Wagner.

192.

Wenn Dir die Kunst auch holde Blumen windet
Zum Kranze, der Dein Haupt so freundlich schmückt,
Wenn Deine Leistung Anerkennung findet,
Und ungetheilter Beifall Dich entzückt! —
So welkt der Lorbeer; Ruhm und Schönheit schwindet;
Nur Liebe ist's, die ewig uns beglückt;
    Darf erst zum Lorbeer sich die Rose neigen,
    Dann nennst Du wahres Glück mit Recht Dein eigen.

Wohl Dir! — Du hast den treuen Freund gefunden,
Der Lust und Leid mit Dir von Herzen theilt;
Und nahen Deinem Leben trübe Stunden,
Als Trost und Schirm an Deiner Seite weilt.
Wenn Neid und Undank je Dein Herz verwunden,
Führt Liebe Dich, die alle Schmerzen heilt;
    Doch wollen Freundeswünsche auch begleiten
    Den Herzensbund, und Segen Euch bereiten.

So wandle, holde Künstlerin durch's Leben,
Indem Dir Kunst und Liebe Blumen streu'n;
Recht lang' mögst Du, die Grazien umschweben,
Noch Königsberg durch Dein Talent erfreu'n.
Du kannst dem Bild des Dichters Leben geben,
Wir müssen selbst, als „Stumme" Dank Dir weih'n:
    So mög' uns Deines Geistes schönes Walten
    In mancher Blüthe herrlich sich entfalten.

Wenn dann Dein Gatte hier im Reich der Töne
Uns leitet in der Harmonien Land;
So stellst Du uns des hohen Dichters Schöne
Lebendig dar im Bild', das er erfand.
Daß manchen Dichter auch der Lorbeer kröne,
Reicht ihm der Künstler gern die Bruderhand;
    Was Schiller, Göthe, Lessing Hohes sangen,
    Mög' oft durch Dich als Wahrheit uns umfangen.

Königsberg, den 24. November 1836.

1

1 Hans Thoma (1839–1924): "The armed Brünnhilde". Original pastel (1896)

2 Dog-whip for Wagner's Newfoundland Russ, framed and decorated as a votive picture

3 Gold watch presented by Richard Wagner to his godson, Wilhelm Stocker, to celebrate the birth of Siegfried Wagner (1869)

4 Franz Stassen (1869–1949): Richard Wagner's grave in Bayreuth. Original oil painting (1916)

5 Ferdinand Leeke (1859–1931), "Wotan's Farewell". Original oil painting (1920)

6 Wilhelm Beckmann (1852–1942): "Richard Wagner in Bayreuth", original oil painting (1880). The picture shows from left to right: Cosima Wagner, Richard Wagner, Franz Liszt and Hans Paul von Wolzogen, editor and publisher of the "Bayreuther Blätter"

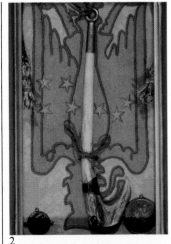

2

3

4

5

6

1883 **1933**

Das Liebesverbot 4. Mai

Parsifal 18. Juni

Rienzi 7. Mai

Götter Dämmerung 14. Juni

Der fliegende Holländer 10. Mai

Siegfried 11. Juni

Tannhäuser (Pariser Fassung) 14. Mai

Die Walküre 9. Juni

Lohengrin 25. Mai

Das Rheingold 7. Juni

Die Meistersinger von Nürnberg 30. Mai

Tristan und Isolde 28. Mai

Wagner in der Zyklus

Staatsoper
Unter den Linden
Einmalige chronologische Aufführung
sämtlicher Werke

Es werden Sonderabonnements zu 12 oder 6 Vorstellungen ausgegeben
Stammabonnenten der Oper und des Schauspiels erhalten ermässigte Zusatzabonnements
Nähere Auskunft und Anmeldungen im Abonnementsbüro, Berlin W 8, Oberwallstraße 22
Fernsprecher: A 6 Merkur 3683

H. J. KALLMANN.

In 1933, the fiftieth anniversary of the death of Richard Wagner, the State Opera "Unter den Linden", Berlin, performed all the Wagner operas with the exception of "Feen". The poster designed for this cycle was the work of the graphic artist H. J. Kallmann

Page 53
Minna Wagner with her dog Peps. Watercolour by Clementine Stockar-Escher, Zurich 1853. Original

54

2

3

Eberhard's Allgemeiner Polizei-Anzeiger, 11 Juny 1853.

Politisch gefährliche Individuen, No 652. Wagner, Richard ehemaliger Kapellmeister aus Dresden, einer der hervorragendsten Anhänger der Umsturzpartei, welcher wegen Theilnahme an der Revolution zu Dresden im May 1849 steckbrieflich verfolgt wird, soll dem Vernehmen nach beabsichtigen, sich von Zürich aus, woselbst er sich gegenwärtig aufhält, nach Deutschland zu begeben. Behufs seiner Habhaftwerdung wird ein Portrait Wagners, der im Betretungsfalle zu verhaften und an das Königl. Stadtgericht zu Dresden abzuliefern sein dürfte, hier beigefügt.

55

4

Mathilde Wesendonck (1828–1902) with her son Guido. Preliminary study for the pastel portrait by Ernst-Benedikt Kietz, Paris/Zurich 1856

Page 57
Mathilde Wesendonck. Marble bust by L. Keiser, Zurich 1860. On the wall: Wagner's original score of the song "Morgen" ("Morning"), 17. 12. 1857, and an original letter from Mathilde

1

1 *Emilie Heim-Müller (1830–1911), wife of the music director Ignaz Heim (1818–1880). Singer and interpreter of Wagnerian rôles. (Pencil sketch by Clementine Stockar-Escher, Zurich 1853)*

2 *Richard Wagner, a copy by A. Brasch, Leipzig, based on an 1867-study, with a dedication to the Lucerne artist Joseph Zelger (1812–1885)*

3 *Richard Wagner's crest, drawn by August Am Rhyn to commemorate the composer's stay in Lucerne*

4 *Richard Wagner's "Beethoven", written at Tribschen in 1870 and published in Leipzig. With dedication: "To his feudal lord Am Rhyn" from "the Tribschen feudal guest Richard Wagner»*

5 *Richard Wagner, bronze bust on a marble plinth, by Friedrich Schaper (1841–1919), circa 1880. (Probably based on a photograph of 1871)*

6 *Handwritten lease of 7th April 1866 for Tribschen, between Walter Ludwig Am Rhyn and Richard Wagner*

2

3

4

5

59

6

1 *Building account from Walter Ludwig Am Rhyn for the alterations made in Tribschen in 1867 (equivalent to more than Sfr. 155,000 by present day standards)*

2 *Richard Wagner: Letter of 15. 10. 1866 to Colonel Am Rhyn (concerning structural alterations connected with the installation of the marble fireplace)*

3 *Richard Wagner, from a photograph, Vienna 1873*

4 *Petroleum lamp from the Wagner household in Tribschen*

Geehrtester Herr Oberst!

Es wäre mir lieb, wenn die Bestellung der Marmorverkleidung des Kamin's, da sie ausserdem die unerwünschte Verzögerung herbeiführt, rückgängig gemacht werden könnte, da ich im Fall, dass Holzauskleidungen mit Möbelplüsch — wie ich ihn besitze — überzogen sich ganz gut ausnimmt. Jedenfalls wünschte ich durch jene Marmorbekleidung, für jetzt meinen Aufenthalt herbeizuführen, und — jene Bestellung nicht rückgängig zu machen — zunächst die Holzbekleidung beachten zu lassen, und die andere erst bei der beabsichtigten vollständigen Einrichtung des Hauses zu verwenden. Somit — Wiederholung meiner dringenden Bitte um grösste Beschleunigung der Heizungsmittelbeschaffung!

Herzlich um Entscheidung für die Benutzung bittend, empfiehlt sich hochachtungsvoll Ihr ebenergebener

Dresden, 15. Oct. 66.

Richard Wagner

2

4

1   Richard Wagner: Letter of complaint to Colonel Am Rhyn, 12th January 1871

2   Richard Wagner: Letter of 7. 8. 1868 to the artist Zelger, inviting him to luncheon on "Sunday at 4 p. m."

3   The Lucerne landscape painter Josef Zelger (1812–1885)

4   Richard Wagner: Libretto of "The Mastersingers of Nuremberg" (Schott, Mainz 1868), with autograph dedication to "Professor Zelger in grateful remembrance"

5   Richard Wagner: Conclusion of his letter of 2. 5. 1869 to the authoress Malwida von Meysenbug (1816– 1903), witness at his wedding to Cosima in Lucerne, 1870

6   Nuremberg Chronicle of Johann Christopherus Wagenseil (1633–1705), with the appendix "Report on the Mastersingers' Art" (1697), source for Wagner's "Meistersinger"

5

63
6

*Richard Wagner:
"Cobbler's Song" from the
Meistersinger "Act II."
(Original)*

Page 65
*Richard Wagner: Photo,
1868, with dedicatory epistle
to the singer Franz Betz,
Munich*

64

Seinem lieben Meistersinger und theuren Freund

Betz

in grosser Freude und zu guten Erinnerung an das vortreffliche Schaffen

Fichtelen bei Luzern.
July 1868.

Richard Wagner

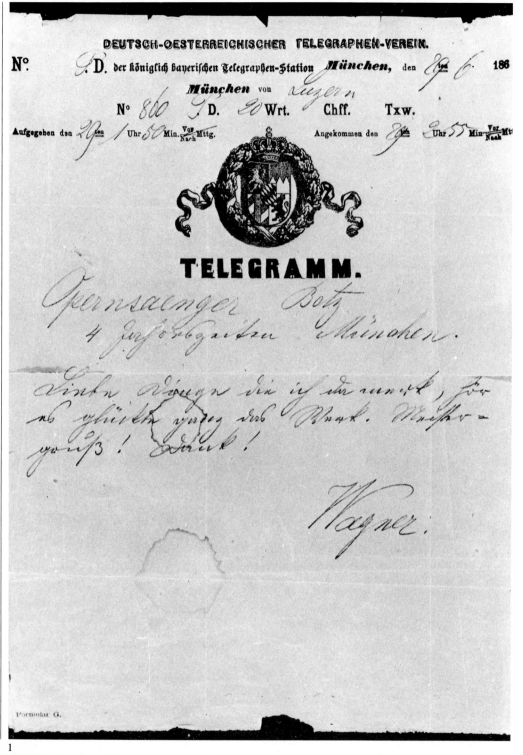

1 *Richard Wagner: Telegram of 29. 6. 1868 to the opera singer Franz Betz (1835–1900) in Munich, first "Hans Sachs" at the premiere of the "Meistersinger" (1868)*

2 *Richard Wagner: Cover of a letter of 26. 7. 1869 to Hans Richter (1843–1916), Munich*

3 *Richard Wagner: Cover of a letter of 6. 4. 1869 to Dr. Ferdinand Leutner, Vienna*

4 *Richard Wagner: Draft sheet of part of Act I of the "Meistersinger" (20. 1. 1867)*

1

1 Vreneli Stocker-Weidmann (1832–1906), Wagner's housekeeper in Munich, Geneva and Lucerne (1864–1872). Photo circa 1882

2 Richard Wagner at the age of 47, Paris, 1860

3+4 Richard Wagner: His designs for a housecoat and trousers, ordered from his Viennese "milliner" Bertha Goldwag (1869)

5 Jakob Stocker (1827–1909), Wagner's servant, married Verena Weidmann in 1867

6 Richard Wagner: Letter of 4. 2. 1868 to Verena Stocker-Weidmann, from Munich announcing his return

7 Cosima Wagner: Letter from Bayreuth to Verena Stocker-Weidmann, 1872–1897 landlady of the restaurant "Neustadt" in Lucerne

2

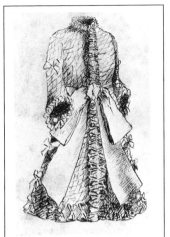

3

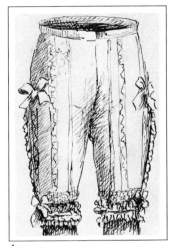

4

5

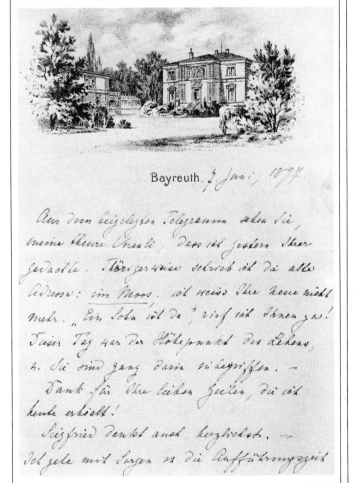

6

7

69

1 Letter of Verena Stocker of 21. 3. 1869 to Wagner's Viennese "milliner" Bertha Goldwag

2 Former study of Richard Wagner, with housecoat, velvet beret and silk shirt of the master

3 Wagner-Museum Library. Right, marble bust of Cosima Wagner by Gustav A. Kietz (1824–1908), 1873 (Copy of the original in Villa Wahnfried). Opposite: Portrait of Franz Liszt

4 Wagner-Museum: View from former dining-room of Richard Wagner into the salon. Left, the triptych by Franz Stassen, right, Stassen's paintings of the grave and the birthplace of Richard Wagner, the marble bust of Mathilde Wesendonck, as well as the pictures "The Daughters of the Rhine" and "Siegfried" by Hans Thoma

2

3

4

1

1 Clothes worn by Wagner in Tribschen

2 Entail "Tripschen", 1788–1931. House built 1627, renovated 1800. Pen drawing by August Am Rhyn, 1908

3 Haus Tribschen, since 1931 now Wagner-Museum (inaugurated 1933), the property of the City of Lucerne. Photo 1983, after the total renovation

4 Libretti of Wagner's music dramas

5 Villa Tribschen, as it was during Wagner's residence there, with the annexe at the side after the extension work 1867

2

3

4

5

*Armchair and dog-whip, part
of the household equipment
belonging to Wagner*

Page 75
*Richard Wagner in the arm-
chair in front of the villa
Tribschen. Photograph
(1867) by Jules Bonnet with
autograph dedication for
Wagner's first biographer
Carl Friedrich Glasenapp
(1847–1915)*

1 Painted table from Wagner's household effects, in front of the fireplace he had had installed, with the "Wagner Encyclopedia" by C. F. Glasenapp, Leipzig 1891

2 New edition, 1869, of two literary productions dating from Wagner's Zurich period (1850/51)

3 Richard Wagner's hand, modelled in plaster by Augusto Benvenuti (1838–1899) in Venice, February 1883

4 Marble bust of Cosima Wagner by Gustav A. Kietz, Bayreuth 1873 (copy)

5 Hans Richter (1843–1916) at the time when he was copying out the "Meistersinger" score in Lucerne (1866/67)

1

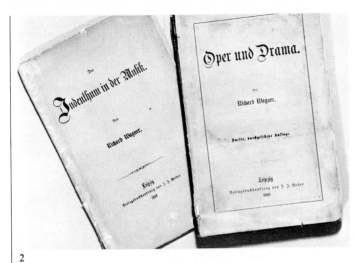

2

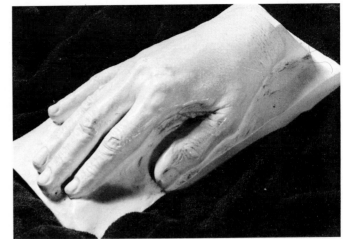

3

4

5

1

1 Single volume copy of all of Wagner's Tribschen writings, bound especially for Cosima and presented to her in 1871

2 Catulle Mendès (1841–1909), Husband of the writer Judith Gautier, Wagner's guest in 1869 and 1870

3 Philippe Auguste Mathias, Comte de Villiers de l'Isle-Adam (1838–1889), visited with French friends Wagner in Lucerne 1869 and 1870

4 Judith Gautier (1846–1917) married to the poet Catulle Mendès from 1868 to 1874, writer, guest in Tribschen 1869 and 1870 as well as in Bayreuth 1876: Wagner's "Muse" for the "Parsifal"

2

3

4

1

1   *Richard Wagner with his daughter Eva and the Newfoundland dog Russ in front of the Villa Tribschen. Photograph by Jules Bonnet, Lucerne, 1867*

2   *Marriage announcement of Richard and Cosima Wagner, 25th August 1870. Sent to Wagner's bookseller Prell, Lucerne*

3   *Copy of the extract from the Registry of Births Lucerne, showing the entry for the birth of Eva Maria von Bülow on 17th February 1867. The extract bears the date 29th April 1909*

Herrn

Prell, Schiffmann'sche Buchhandlung

Luzern.

Wir beehren uns, hiermit unsere am 25. August d. J. in der protestantischen Kirche zu Luzern vollzogene Trauung anzuzeigen.

Richard Wagner.
Cosima Wagner, geb. Liszt.

2

Schweiz. Eidgenossenschaft.   Form. Nr. 7.

Civilstandskreis Luzern.

Copie
~~Auszug~~ aus dem Geburts-Register.
(Geburtschein.)

Kanton Luzern.

Band _____ Seite _____

Den *siebzehnten Februar* _____ eintausend acht hundert *siebenund sechzig* _____ um *zehn* Uhr _____ Minuten _____ Vor mittags wurde geboren zu **Luzern**, *Fritschein* _____ von *Bülow Eva Maria* _____ eheliche Tochter des *Hans von Bülow* _____ Beruf: *königl. Hofkapellmeister* von *Preussen* _____ wohnhaft in *Luzern* _____ und der *Cosima, Franziska Liszt* _____ von _____

Für richtigen Auszug
Luzern, den *29. April* 190*9*

Der Civilstandsbeamte:

Vide Randbemerkung: Rückseite

81

3

1

VILLA
TRIEBSCHEN.
Diner zur Feier des 4. September 1870.

Potage crème d'orge.

Truites au bleu sauce hollandaise.
Pommes de terre.

Filet de bœuf à la jardinière.

Canards à la milanaise.
Petits pâtés à la Reine.

Pois fin à la française.

Chapon truffé.
Salade verte aux œufs.

Charlotte russe

Dessert: Divers. Fruits.

2

3

1   Johann Heinrich Tschudi, pastor of the Protestant parish of Lucerne from 1863 to 1874. Celebrated the marriage between Richard Wagner and Cosima and baptised Siegfried Wagner in St. Matthew's Church (1870)

2   Menu of banquet given on the baptismal day of the Wagner-offspring Siegfried (1869–1930) on 4th September 1870

3   Cosima von Bülow (1837–1930) 1857, shortly after the marriage to Hans von Bülow

4   The Reformed Church of St. Matthew Lucerne. Wood engraving after a plan by Ferdinand Stadler, Zurich (1860)

5   Letter of Richard Wagner of 25th August 1871 to Pastor Johann Heinrich Tschudi, who had officiated at the wedding of Wagner and Cosima in the Protestant church of St. Matthew a year before

4

Hochgeehrter Herr Pastor!

Erlauben Sie mir, in dankbarer
Erinnerung an den segensvollen Akt
meiner Trauung mit meiner lieben Frau;
welche heute vor einem Jahr durch Sie
so theilnahmvoll vollzogen wurde,
Sie zu ersuchen, das beiliegende kleine
Geschenk von fünfzig Franken zum
Besten der hiesigen, Ihrer Fürsorge
übergebenen reformirten Gemeinde
gütigst in Verwendung bringen zu wollen.
Mit aufrichtiger Hochschätzung
empfehle ich mich Ihnen mit meiner Frau
zu geneigtem Angedenken, und verbleibe
Ihr

ergebener
Richard Wagner

Triebschen
25 August 1871

F. Luckhardt

K.u.K. HOF-PHOTOGRAPH
·–·–· WIEN ·–·–·

1

1   Photograph of Richard and Cosima Wagner. F. Luckhardt, 9th May 1872, Vienna

2   Concert programme, 10. 3. 1875, on the concert given in Budapest conducted by Liszt and Wagner (first public appearance together since 1865 in St. Gallen)

3+4   Caricatures of Franz Liszt (Budapest 1875)

5   Franz Liszt (1811–1886), lithograph 1830, with the signature "Liszt Ferency"

6   Franz Liszt in his study in Weimar. Photograph by Louis Held, Weimar

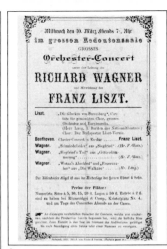

2

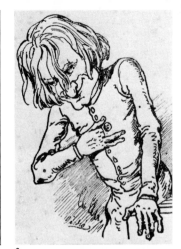

3

4

5

6

1

2

3

1 King Ludwig II. as Lohengrin beneath the Wagner moon (caricature from the comic paper "Floh" (flea), Vienna 1885

2 Bohemian glass goblet, gift of Ludwig II. to Richard Wagner

3 King Ludwig II. (1845–1886), portrait of him as a young man, 1865

4 Letter of King Ludwig II. to Cosima Wagner (probably June 1869)

5 Wagner's Erard grand piano (gift 1858 of the widow of the Parisian instrument-maker of German descent) and album leaf E flat for Frau Betty Schott, Mainz (1875)

6 Frau Betty Schott (1821–1875), wife of Wagner's main publisher

7 Wagner's main publisher from 1859, Franz Philipp Schott, Mainz (1811–1874)

8 Richard Wagner, 1870 photo (with handwritten signature)

4

5

6

7

8

1

2

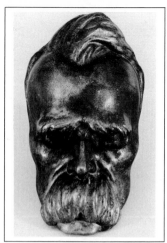

3

1 *Portrait of Friedrich Nietzsche (1844–1900), Pforta 1865*

2 *Friedrich Nietzsche 1870*

3 *Death-mask of Nietzsche (1900), bronze*

4 *Letter of Nietzsche to Wagner from Basel, 18th Nov. 1871*

5 *Envelope with address (written by Nietzsche) and date stamp "Basel, 15. 7. 1878" to Wagner's friend Mathilde Maier, Mainz (1833–1910)*

6 *Richard Wagner in the circle of his friends in Villa Wahnfried Bayreuth. Wood engraving after an oil painting by Georg Papperitz (1880)*

7 *Nietzsche first editions*

4

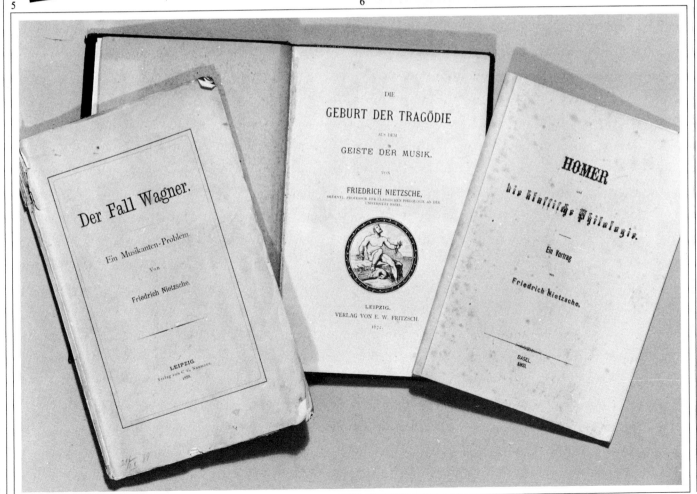

1 Richard Wagner: *Siegfried Idyll* (1870), page 3 of the final score, facsimile autograph (Munich 1923)

2 The former public house Dubeli, Furrengasse, Lucerne, Richard Wagner's favourite pub. Photograph by Franz Schneider, Lucerne (1932)

3 Letter of Hans von Bülow (1830–1894) of 2. 4. 1866 to the singer Franz Betz, Munich

4 The Wagner corner in the former public house Dubeli. Photograph by Franz Schneider, Lucerne (1932)

2

'conditio sine qua non' meiner verantwortlichen Annahme des
kgl. Auftrags, ich bin kein eiteiltlicher Hofkapellmeister und
betrachte dessen Erfüllung als eine Künstlerische Ehrensache
so daß ich lediglich aus diesem Grunde meine Aus=Reise ver=
schoben und die Direktion des Sobuger Musikfestes im Juni
abgelehnt habe.

Entschuldigen Sie gütigst die Flüchtigkeit dieser Zeilen, die sich
aus meiner Arbeitsüberhäuftheit u.s.w. so wie aus dem Wunsche
erklärt, Sie nicht auf Antwort warten zu lassen und empfan=
gen Sie unter Wiederholung meines Dankes für Ihre freundli=
chen Gesinnungen in Betreff unserer Sache wie meiner Person
die Versicherung meiner hochachtungsvollen Ergebenheit.

München, 2. April 1866   Ihrer v. Bülow

3

91

4

der Luzerner Feuerwehr, die sich bei einem Brande als tüchtig bewährte, schrieb Wagner am 8. November 1869 einen kurzen Männerchor:

Treu - e sei uns're Zier,

Lie - be sei das Pa - nier, Tat - kraft un - ser

Wort, Gott un - ser höch - ster Hort!

Gott un - ser Hort!

128

1

2

1   *Richard Wagner, Motto for the Lucerne Fire Brigade (8. 11. 1869), identical with the one he wrote for the German Fire Brigade*

2   *Lucerne in Richard Wagner's day. Photograph by Adolphe Braun, Dornach*

3   *Tribschen, contemporary photograph by Jules Bonnet before the alterations of 1867*

4   *Hans Thoma (1839–1924): "Daughters of the Rhine" Watercolour (1896)*

3

Wagner's Erard grand piano with the pianoforte arrangement of "Siegfried" prepared by Karl Klindworth (1830–1916) for Schott, Mainz (Dedication of 14. 8. 1871 to the Wesendonck, Zurich), and a sheet of the fair copy of the score made by Hans Richter

Page 95
Hans Thoma (1839–1924): "Norns", watercolour (1896)

1

1 Edmund Herger (1860–
1907): "Wotan's Entry".
Reproduction of a painting
(circa 1900)

2 The Wagner daughters
with Siegfried and Hans
Richter (circa 1890)

3 Announcement of the
Bayreuth Festival 1882 with
the premiere of "Parsifal"

4 Richard Wagner posing
for his portraitist Auguste
Renoir 1882

5 The Bayreuth Festival
Theatre at the time of the
first festival (1876) still without its «royal edifice»

6 Emil Heckel (1831–
1908) founded in Mannheim
the first Wagner Association,
1871, the composer presenting his report to it in 1872

7 Wagner's appeal for
support for the Bayreuth
festival concept (1871)

2

3

4

97

5

BERICHT
an den
Deutschen Wagner-Verein
über die
Umstände und Schicksale,
welche die Ausführung des Bühnenfestspieles
»Der Ring des Nibelungen«
begleiteten.
Von
Richard Wagner.

Leipzig,
Commissions-Verlag von E. W. Fritzsch.

6

UEBER DIE AUFFÜHRUNG
DES
BÜHNENFESTSPIELES
DER RING DES NIBELUNGEN.
EINE
MITTHEILUNG UND AUFFORDERUNG
AN DIE
FREUNDE SEINER KUNST
VON
RICHARD WAGNER.

LEIPZIG,
VERLAG VON E. W. FRITZSCH.

7

1

2

3

4

5